Acclaim for Ellen Pendleton's
READ & RUN

"Ellen's first book is exciting reading from cover to cover. It made me feel like I was right there camping and hiking and riding the river right through Ellen's eyes. It is honest, a learning experience, and most of all, it made me wonder what was going to happen next!"

— Donna Murphy, Carmel CA USA

". . . a reflection of a sensitive woman's journey through a magnificent alpine landscape in which Ellen brings to the reader a deep appreciation of nature and its spiritual essence."

— Patrick Kraft, Carmel CA USA

"Ellen's first book allows you to enter her soul literally by using twisting paths, rugged terrain and rapid water as symbolic of her life's personal journey. Amazing, how she holistically blends every facet of life into the moment — instantly captivating you to the point of easily being drawn into the action of nature's natural selection or awesome meditative silence of night in the wilderness. Knowing that action and silence are one in the same, she conveys this with sincere simplicity, the very quality which allows her to co-exist with nature as one of its own. Something many of us may never learn in this lifetime."

— Joseph Lucido, Monterey CA USA

". . . a wonderful journey through a life less simple than mine and definitely more exciting. A glimpse into the thoughts and workings of a mind full of passion and wonder with a view of ourselves few of us dare to talk about much less write about.

". . . the feelings I got most from the book were one of respect and admiration. Ellen went through a lot in that first book and was ever so kind to share with us. We all have experiences in life but few of us are able to convey with such thoughtfulness and insight. A trip into a life not our own, but one not far from the possibility of being our own."

— alanb, Ojai CA USA

READ & RUN

READ & RUN

by
Ellen Pendleton

READ & RUN

Earth Travels
by Ellen Pendleton

Previously published as MY FIRST BOOK

Front cover photograph: ©Michael J. McDonald,
Lone Pine Lake, California USA

Back cover photograph: ©CW Freedman

Mount Whitney photographs: ©Michael J. McDonald

Printed in USA by CreateSpace.com

www.Earth-Travels.net

Published by
espbooks
P.O. Box 221238
Carmel CA 93922 USA
www.espbooks.net

This book is dedicated with
LOVE, JOY and GRATITUDE
to my children

Sunshine
Jeremiah
Aja

my teachers, angels, heroes, friends,
inspiration and motivation.

*I never travel without my diary. One should always
have something sensational to read.*
— Oscar Wilde

CONTENTS

I should not talk so much about myself if there were
anybody else whom I knew as well.
— Henry David Thoreau, *Walden*

Trust Thyself

Trust thyself; every heart vibrates to that iron string.
Insist on yourself; never imitate.
That which each can do best,
None but his Maker can teach him.

There is a time in every man's education
When he arrives at the conviction that imitation is suicide;
that he must take himself for better, or worse, as his portion.

The power which resides in him is new in Nature
and none but he knows what that is which he can do,
nor does he know until he has tried.
— Ralph Waldo Emerson

PART I — *Rogue River, Oregon*

June 21, Wednesday
Sun ☼ Gemini Ⅱ / Moon ☽ Aries ♈
The Rogue River, Day One

"Let the wild ruckus begin."
— to misquote Maurice Sendak
from *Where the Wild Things Are*

The river is beautiful and the morning perfect. Larry and Michael take off. Mac backpaddles so he can watch. On the first big wave Larry and Michael's boat flips. Mac's adrenaline kicks in and the fear leaves his body when he sees the child in the water. Off he goes immediately to assist in the rescue.

Larry pops up and grabs onto the ducky (a bright yellow, inflatable kayak). Where's Michael? Brooke's boat sits off in an eddy with everybody aboard watching and yelling. A little yellow helmet bobs up and down, visible between the waves. Oh man, . . . would I ever bring my kids on a whitewater river run? Mac provides enough to worry about.

We take off, the sweep boat, ready to pick up swimmers, paddles or boats. It feels strange without a paddle. All I can do is watch, pray and cheer them on. Larry and Michael swim over to Brooke's boat. Mac runs the rapid like a pro. I reach down and rescue a stray paddle. My own fear of the river ride was replaced by concern about that little boy riding those nasty waves. Thank goodness he's safe. Our boat joins the others.

"What a blast! Let's do that again," Michael bubbles up with an obviously different response than mine.

Larry is out of breath but in great humor. "We never got into sync. It happened so fast. I paddled one way, he paddled the other and over we went. It's not as easy as it looks."

"Are you okay?" looking at Michael. "I was worried about you."

"I was worried," Larry inserts, "but he was bobbing up and down screaming, *Yee-hah!* and *Whoopie!* He was having a blast. I tried to grab onto him, but he bobbed around then he finally grabbed onto the ducky and we floated over here."

Elaine, the mom, does not look happy. This trip probably wasn't her idea.

Our boat got soaked from that last rush of waves. Thighs, shins, shoulders, faces, and arms get reapplied with sunscreen. I offer some to Randy and the boys. Randy wants to get some sun and the boys have their own sunscreen. Getting sunburned is not on my list.

"Randy, what was the name of that rapid?" I ask.

"Oh, I don't think it has a name."

Everyone seems to be fine. Michael climbs back in Brooke's boat and we paddle on to the next rapid and the next.

We travel a couple of miles then stop for lunch under the Grave Creek Bridge.

"This is the last bit of road we'll see until take-out. Everything from here on is legislated *Wild & Scenic River*," Randy inserts. "This is where the river begins."

"What was all of that?" referring to the last two hours on the river.

"Oh that's nothing. Those were just riffles. Now the fun begins." Randy likes being head guide and he's good at it. "Grave Creek is where most folks put in their boats. Up ahead is Grave Creek Falls, Rainie Falls and Tyee Rapid. We'll stop at Rainie Falls and scout it. Everyone will get out. Brooke and Jenn will run the Fish Ladder to the right side. This is Jenn's first Rogue run as a new *Echo* guide so she's running the whole trip solo without passengers. Mac and Larry can decide whether or not to run the Fish Ladder when we get there. Anybody for GORP?" Randy pulls out a gallon-sized plastic bag full of Good Old Raisins, Peanuts and M&M's® and hands it to me. He gives us some shore-side instructions, points to the outhouse location and directs us to Jenn for the hand-washing lesson. I pick out the raisins and nuts to eat while the kids pick out the M&M's®. The kids pay close attention to Jenn as she instructs us concerning the environmentally correct method of wilderness cleanliness. Jenn has a pierced tongue. The kids stare at it and whisper. With the lesson complete the kids run off to play in the crystal clear creek and look for "the grave." The guides go to work on lunch.

An osprey circles overhead, dives straight down into the water and comes up with a fish. The kids ask mom and dad about the pierced tongue.

"Ask her. I'm sure it's okay to ask Jenn questions," mom and dad say.

"Watch, he'll probably circle again and show off his catch," Randy offers his osprey expertise.

Sure enough, the bird circles and displays his prize, a good-sized fish!

The kids find Jenn, circle her and ask away.

I climb into Mac's ducky to get the feel. I take it out, stay close to shore and away from the current. The upcoming Grave Creek Falls is a Class III and Rainie Falls is a Class V. Randy says that Rainie might be closer to a Class VI because it's a high water year. Class VI must be portaged. I don't know if I'm ready for a ducky yet. I'm not ready to make such big decisions. A lake. A ducky on a lake might be good to try first. The river moves fast and I don't know what's up ahead and what to do when. Fear. The front of the oar boat with the teenage brothers Dreux and Loren, will do just fine to enjoy myself and watch Mac learn.

Within minutes the hors d'oeuvres are ready. We are each given our own gray plastic *Echo* mug with our name written on the bottom and the responsibility of keeping track of it for four days. Two large drink containers take center stage on the table. One is a five-gallon size, like the Gatorade®-type in football games, full of water. And the other is a three-gallon size full of juice.

Today is a Deli Lunch Day and I make mine vegetarian. The ice chest sits full of sodas, lots of sodas. No white sugar for me and no caffeine. I retrieve the empty juice container from the trash, read the ingredients list, give it a thumbs up and pass on the chocolate chip cookies.

The men's group that we saw in the Galice Café last night and this morning, starts paddling by. First, an oar boat floats by loaded with plenty of gear, supplies and one oarsman. Then solos parade by: duckies, hard-bodied kayaks, inner tubes and other small crafts. Then two paddle by in a canoe. Oh, such a variety. They cruise and wave. The river has a way of instantly transforming middle-aged men magically into little boys. Just put them in a boat and add water. Following all comes the sweep boat oared by two men and loaded with more gear.

After our lunch the guides clean up and load the gear. Rainie Falls, a designated Class V, (VI in some publications), is up soon and Larry decides to ride in the oar boat. No one else is up for a ducky ride, besides Mac, so Randy deflates Larry's ducky. We all take off.

Rainie Falls. As we approach the roar grows louder before the falls become visible. All boats pull over to the left bank.

"Everybody out," Randy guides. "And keep your life jackets on."

We pile out and remind the young ones to be aware of the poison oak. Other folks are also on the trail to check out Rainie Falls. Here's its description from the book *Western Whitewater, From the Rockies to the Pacific* by Jim Cassady, Bill Cross and Fryar Calhoun:

Rainie Falls (V). Named for "Old Man Rainie" who lived here and gaffed salmon at the falls. <u>Recognition:</u> A horizon line at the end of a long pool warns boaters to pull over. Scout from either bank; the left offers better views, but boaters must then ferry back to the right to run, line, or portage. <u>The rapid:</u> Most of the river drops over a 12' ledge on the left into a chaotic hydraulic. Though boaters occasionally run the main falls, most pick one of two alternate chutes to the right. The "Fish Ladder," an artificial channel blasted down the far right, is shallow and rocky but provides a route for running or lining moderate-sized boats (difficult at low flows). Portages are along its right bank. The middle chute, a narrow Class IV staircase, carries enough water for larger boats, but its tricky entrance involves a close approach to the worst part of the main falls. Above 2,000 cfs or so the risk of being swept over the main falls increases. Scout carefully from shore; the middle chute's entrance is difficult to see from river level. Also, beware of bridging in its abrupt, jarring drops.

The men's group who cruised by earlier also scouts Rainie. Randy decides to run it straight down the middle by himself.

"Are you kidding?" I'm concerned.

Randy guides, "I'll pick you up downstream. Brooke, Jenn and Mac will run the Fish Ladder."

We all watch from the shore as one of the large gear boats from the men's group approaches the falls with two passengers.

"They look a little too far left," comments Randy.

We watch. Watching another boat on the river is *almost* as fun as running it. They get closer to the drop. And closer, . . . and over the falls they go. Both men become airborne, lifting off of their seats, separating from their raft. Water splashes everywhere. The men plop down and land back in the boat. Cheers erupt. The two men paddle furiously to get away from the falls. Somehow, they circle back. The boat sits motionless. Then the boat turns and brushes back into the falls. The men resume their furious paddling.

"They're caught in a back eddy," Randy claims. "The current pulls them around in a counterclockwise direction back into the falls again."

About the third or fourth paddling frenzy, they successfully liberate themselves and continue downstream. The men's other gear boat approaches. This one is going for the right side of the main falls.

"There's a serious hole there. I wouldn't go that way. See all of the different currents there?" Randy points out the chaos.

The boat sneaks up slowly, . . . floats up to the ledge, then rolls over the falls.

"Man, they're going over!" Randy prepares for a possible rescue. Their boat fills with water, narrowly misses a boulder on their right then spins around. We take pictures.

They stay in the boat! They survive Rainie Falls. Mac agrees that this would not be a good ducky run. Fun is one thing but he's not stupid. The guides plus Mac head back toward their boats. We're instructed to sit back, watch from the shore and meet them downstream.

Randy runs it first. He positions himself center, straight down the tongue. I hold my breath. I can't believe he's going to do it. Here he comes. I get out the camera. He backpaddles, backpaddles, . . . then . . . boom! . . . over the falls he goes. I almost forget to take a picture. Beautiful, he did it! Beautiful. Quickly he maneuvers the boat to the opposite shore where the Fish Ladder comes out. We break into applause.

Mac is upriver. His run will be across the current to the north shore, across the river from us, and into the Fish Ladder. I couldn't help him if I wanted. I just have to sit here across the river and watch.

It seems like it takes forever for them appear. What is the holdup?

Finally we see a boat emerge from behind the foliage. It's Brooke. She runs the Fish Ladder and almost makes it to rejoin the main river. Suddenly, her boat turns sideways and stops. We're across the river, so we don't have a clear view but it appears that she's perched on a couple of rocks and stuck. She stands up and bounces, trying to free her boat.

Mac rounds the bend and we hear Randy yelling. Mac stops behind Brooke's boat. Randy yells again. Mac gets out of his boat and climbs into Brooke's boat. They both work at trying to get the boat free. It's not budging. I take pictures but can't see much. Randy throws a line. They pull, they push, they jump and eventually they free the boat. Mac's ducky runs off by itself and Randy pulls it in. Jenn follows, bumps through the shallow run and goes after Mac's boat. We cheer. Brooke, Randy and Mac ferry across to pick us up.

The Rogue seems to be a friendly river. Moods vary from gentle and soft, to furiously challenging, to playful and fun, to gracious and exalted. After the occasional splashing I remind the boys, "YoMama says reapply your sunscreen."

During the calm stretches, Randy, Dreux, Loren and I have plenty of time for conversation: "How many times have you run the Rogue? Where do you live? How did you get started? What do you do during the winter?"

"Where do you go to school? What do you study? Have you ever rafted a river before? How'd you decide on the Rogue?"

"What do you do for a living? You have how many children? How long have you and Mac been together?"

Questions are asked and answered. Conversation gets put on hold during rapids then resumes during the calm. Randy lives in Colorado. This may be his last season as a guide because he's developing a solar-based company. He says, "The Rogue is my favorite river. The mountains in Colorado are so steep that the rivers run fast and furious. There's hardly any time between rapids. If you fall out, you might swim a long haul before anyone could pick you up."

The brothers have an interesting scenario. Their mother's birthday is coming up this week. To celebrate, Dad took Mom to the Caribbean and has completely planned the entire week for the boys that includes this four-day river trip.

"Where are you off to next?"

"I don't know. The itinerary is in the car," they answer. Bed and breakfast reservations have been made, maps routed and clocked, suggestions for restaurants, and sights to see along the way. What a great way to avoid a teenage "kegger" party at the house; send them on a four-day rafting trip and beyond. Dreux, the older brother, has a handicapped wrist and hand. He's missing a thumb.

The weather is perfect, not a cloud in the sky. Temperature is probably 80°, no wind. We take turns jumping overboard as a refreshing break from the heat. Mac doesn't have to submerge; he sits so low in the water that he gets wet during almost every rapid. During calm stretches he sometimes takes his helmet off and uses it as a bucket to wet his head. Mac loves cold water. I'm not that fond of cold water; I love the heat.

"Hey, Big Mac, great run. You're getting it," Randy encourages.

Mid-afternoon Randy signals to the left bank, Doe Bar. This will be our home for the night. Randy seems elated that it's vacant. After so many years running a river, guides know special places to set up camp. He also says it has a great bathroom.

Doe Bar is a lovely sandy beach. We unload the drybags, each finding our own, and get our tents from the tent bag. I have to go to the bathroom really bad. "Where is it?"

"Up there," Randy points to the hillside woods.

Still in my life jacket, I run up the hill, look for the bathroom but see nothing. Was he kidding? I find a spot where the others can't see me and go tinkle. Maybe it's a great bathroom because of the outstanding view. An osprey appears for some afternoon fishing and some Canada geese gather on the opposite shore.

I venture upstream a bit, jump in the chilly water to float downstream practicing the recommended position for swimming if you get tossed out of the boat. "Keep your feet up, outstretched in front of you. Don't drag your feet or have them behind your body. Foot entrapment is a leading killer in whitewater," the safety talk echoes.

Back to camp at Doe Bar, Mac is busy looking for the perfect tent spot. Here is the priority: 1. Level ground, 2. Soft, 3. View of the sunrise and, 4. Close to the action but not too close. Whenever possible we face the tent door east to take advantage of the warm, early morning sun. The priority list is unspoken, formulated from past experience. We find our spot. Dreux and Loren find their spot, not too far away. The guides are busy setting up the kitchen. What a production! The family sets up camp far away from everyone else.

Randy calls us together for the "bathroom" instructions. He takes the hand washing bucket, soap and the strainer cup. He's also carrying one half of a kayak paddle. We all walk across the sand bar toward the woods on the hillside.

"Up that trail," Randy motions, "is a three-sided chemical toilet. Now, . . . nobody likes to be surprised when you're up there doing your thing, so when you go up there, take this paddle with you. That way, if the paddle isn't here, it means someone is up there doing his or her business. Wait right here for whoever is up there to bring the paddle back down. Then it's your turn. Any questions?"

Years of experience probably went into devising the paddle system and I am glad that I wasn't on the ground floor of the research project.

We return to tent duty: Set down the tarp, lay out the tent, send through the poles, fasten the poles. Done. Doe Bar is a nice and sandy beach, so our bed will be soft tonight. We open our drybags. Amazing, everything seems to be perfectly dry. We unzip the tent door and throw in our sleeping bags, Therm-a-Rests®, pillows and clothes bags. We immediately change clothes placing wet shoes and socks next to us on a boulder to make use of the solar energy.

Twelve folding chairs appear circling the evening fire pit. The hors d'oeuvre table is set up, lovely and ready for us to begin nibbling. Lots of cheese, crackers, dips, nuts, some kind of fish in a can, juice, sodas, beer and wine await.

Randy is busy at the barbecue. Jenn and Brooke create in the kitchen. The family constructs two tents. Elaine and Larry issue commands to their troops. Loren and

Dreux struggle with their borrowed tent. Mac offers to help. The boys probably haven't done much camping so far in their lives.

I offer Brooke and Jenn, "Can I help?"

"No thanks, we've got it under control."

And they do. They have the system down. I feel spoiled just waiting for dinner to be served. Yes, the trip cost a lump of money but so far it's worth every penny. I wander off downstream and find an unusual flowering plant that I've never seen before. This is my first trip to Oregon and the plants are different here on the Rogue River than back home. It's so beautiful here.

Back to camp the brothers' tent is up. Mac stands up on the hillside taking panoramic camera shots. Folks are beginning to gather in the designated lounge area. Beth is sitting on her dad's lap. Dreux is relaxed, reading a required book for school, *Their Eyes Were Watching God* by Zora Neale Hurston. Davey talks to Randy, the barbecue master. Elaine is organizing inside their tent. Bringing three kids and all of their paraphernalia has got to be quite a production. No boom boxes, headphones or electronic games; good. Michael "pitters" down by the water; apparently building something. It's still warm even though the sun is starting to dip behind the hills. The time to do nothing feels divine.

Dinner is excellent. Being a vegetarian I pass on the chicken and steak. Brooke's mashed potatoes are the best ever. They're full of red onions, herbs, garlic, and chunks of goodies. There's corn on the cob and a huge salad. Mac photographs his full plate.

After cooking, Randy moves the barbecue pit to the lounge area. "Red wine or white?" he asks.

That's service. What fun it is to sit around the fire and eat such a lovely meal. It's been a good day. Dessert, too, strawberry shortcake.

"Is there any white sugar in the strawberries?" assuming that the shortcake has it.

"No," Jenn gleams, "and none in the whipping cream."

Hallelujah. Happy camper.

After dinner I insist on helping with the dishes. They can't believe it but I love to do dishes when I go camping. The guides resist until I insist. It's the hot soapy water. I love bubble baths and doing dishes is the closest I get to a bubble bath while out in the wilds. Also, it helps keep my hands warm and fingernails clean.

"I found a plant downstream. Can you help identify it?" I ask.

"I have my *Audubon Field Guide to North American Wildflowers*. We can look for the plant after chores," Jenn gives.

After dishes, I run off to use the "bathroom." The paddle is missing, so I wait. Elaine walks down the trail and passes the baton (the paddle). I wander up. And up. *Hey, where does this little trail go?* Exploring a little further, . . . sure enough, there really *is* a chemical toilet with toilet paper and everything. Randy wasn't joking.

The kids are atop a boulder overlooking a little creek. A deer has wandered in close to the kitchen. A doe. That's probably why they call this Doe Bar. The kids frantically warn me, "Sh-sh-sh. Don't scare it away. Move slowly. Be quiet."

Randy snickers and whispers softly to the adults only, "We call them Rogue Rodents. Just *try* to get rid of it."

I know what he means. Many, many years ago the kids and I camped at Lake Almanor in Northern California, for about five days. Deer wandered through camp. At first the deer seemed like rare and amazing delicate wild creatures. Then in the middle of the night they raided our camp, dumping over ice chests and rummaging through anything that smelled like food. They behaved like a combination raccoon, bear, and town dog. I remember running through the campground in the moonlight, half-dressed, chasing those "lovely docile critters" out of our camp. (I also learned to put food safely away. Duh!)

Jenn appears with the wildflower field guide in hand. "Where is it?" And off we go. Beth and Davey ask to come along. We walk downstream to try and find the plant.

"Here it is."

Jenn, obviously experienced, thumbs quickly through the guide. While leafing through the pages she explains the organizational system and says, "Is this it?" She bends down holding the guide next to our discovery, *Showy Milkweed*. We compare picture with the real thing. Jenn reads the comment section,

> *There are recipes for preparing this species as a vegetable, but the plants should be positively identified as some of the Milkweeds are highly poisonous, and eating them can result in death.*

It's a good thing we already had dinner.

We return to the fire pit lounge area as the sun slips behind the hills. Surprisingly, there seems to be no major mosquito problem. Perfect weather. *And* it's the first day of summer. Oh, what a perfect day it has been.

Fireside conversation begins as stars replace the daylight. Mac sits surrounded by the children. Everyone asks questions of everyone else. Stories get told; questions get asked and answered. Games are played. Kids get warned about staying away from the fire. Michael seems to be part pyromaniac.

Davey emerges with a special talent. You know when you're around a fire, sometimes the smoke gets right in your face and you have to move? Then it'll go away and you can return to your spot? Well, Davey seems to have a knack for directing the smoke. I watch him silently at first. Then I mention it to him, "How do you move the smoke?"

He twinkles with appreciated recognition and the smoke blows right into my face.

"Davey," I coax, hoping to imply that I'm on his side and please keep the smoke out of my face.

He looks at Dreux and the smoke blows that direction. Nobody else seems to be picking up on this little game. Maybe nobody else believes it possible. Davey offers a few more demonstrations and I decide to keep on his good side.

"I can make the smoke go where I want it to," Davey announces to the group.

"Sure you can," sarcasm from Michael. The smoke blows into Michael's face.

Davey lets out a scary laugh and says, "I'm the Fire Master," and follows it with another laugh. Others get into it, calling it luck and refusing to believe. A few of us watch without comment.

I sit, stretching backwards, watching the stars. A shooting star passes by and flickers out. I watch for more.

Bedtime comes soon. One by one and two by two, campers bid goodnight and slip off to their tents. Mac and I are the last guests up. My neck is getting tired from stargazing. The guides pick a spot between the kitchen and the river, lay out a big tarp, roll out their bags, and, . . . that's it — no tent. This would make stargazing a lot easier on the neck.

Dreux and Loren shuffle around in the dark. Loren appears, "Can I borrow a flashlight for a minute?"

"Sure. Don't you have one?" I ask.

"No. We forgot it."

"Here," handing him a flashlight. He does what he does and brings it back in a few minutes. Mac hands him a little squeeze key chain model flashlight in return. "Here, we've got an extra."

"Thanks."

They are so cute, brothers camping together. I imagine my three kids on a four-day rafting trip together and laugh. The guides whisper and giggle under the starlight. They sure put in a long day at the office. But just look at their office . . . .

June 22, Thursday ☼ Cancer ♋ / ◯ Taurus ♉
The Rogue River, Day Two

May what I do flow from me like a river, no forcing and no holding back, the way it is with children.
— Rainer Maria Rilke

The light of day yawns, stretches and wakes me up. I always wake up early when camping. At home I can easily sleep till nine or ten o'clock, but out here I'm up with the dawn's early light. Ah-h, . . . the sunrise. No one else stirs, so I stay quiet and watch the morning unfold. Water birds travel downstream.

When sufficiently entertained by the beauty, I lie down and meditate. Meditating out-of-doors in a wilderness environment is comforting. My best meditations occur out in the wilds. The riversong, especially, soothes my soul.

When I come back, I notice Beth off by herself down by the water. I join her and ask if she would like some company. She's watching some baby fish. She's such a doll. She's the youngest, seven. Davey just turned nine and Michael is eleven.

Breakfast is nummy. French toast, yogurt, GrapeNuts®, and melons. Loren appears. Someone snores. "Loren, is Dreux still sleeping?" I ask. Sure enough, he is still in the sack.

Dry bags have to be ready to load by 9 a.m. Breakdown. The whole family has quite a production to orchestrate. Beth hangs around the shoreline solo and I join her again.

Load 'em up and let's go. Loren, Dreux and I retake our positions at the front of the sweep boat and slather up with sunscreen. The boys got sunburned yesterday, so they put a towel across their legs. Mac climbs into his ducky and the family boards Brooke's boat. Ah, another day in paradise.

The next rapid is Tyee Rapids, Class IV. Brooke briefs Mac. Off we go.

Soon after launch, Mac flips. My heart drops. I panic. Mac's helmet pops up close to the ducky. He grabs onto his boat, rides the rapid and his helmet bobs up and down between the waves. I say a prayer. Randy doesn't seem rattled but I fear hypothermia. Mac doesn't have on a wet suit.

Flashback: Last April, Mac participated in swift water rescue drills on the Upper Kern River in California, as part of the *Outdoor Adventures* River Guide Training course. His boat flipped and he floated down the river. The water was freezing cold snowmelt. Everyone wore wetsuits. Fortunately other guides were practicing the Throw Bag Rescue technique downstream. The first few missed him, but somebody finally bagged him. They pulled him out and set him down at a picnic table. Hypothermia was beginning to set in and he wouldn't stop shivering. He couldn't catch his breath. The guides wrapped him in blankets, vigorously rubbed him all over and gave him some hot chocolate to drink trying to warm him up from the inside out.

But this is mid-June and the water is certainly warmer here than the Kern last April. My eyes follow him closely, "Where's Mac? Where's Mac?" I hold my breath until I see him reach the other boats.

I hang on tight as we run Tyee, not thinking of us, only eager to get to Mac.

"Are you okay?" I ask when we reach him.

"Yeah. When I came up the boat was right there and I grabbed on to it. I felt that shock when I hit the cold water but I'm okay."

He probably had Kern River flashbacks, too.

Brooke briefs Mac on the next rapid, Wildcat Rapids, Class III. Randy signals the go-ahead and Brooke takes off. Jenn goes next and then Mac hesitates, waiting to see how the other two run it.

"Learn to sit upriver, read the flow of the rapid, then run it," Randy advises Mac. "You can do it. Read and run."

Mac takes off and immediately disappears between waves again; I hold my breath. Mac executes Wildcat perfectly. We follow. Randy positions the boat and hits a wave. Dreux gets especially wet. WAKE UP!

We float through a calm, flat area and I snap photos of the children taking turns with the oars. Randy lets me give the oars a try, jumps into the river to cool off then climbs back in.

"Hey, these oars are heavy! How do you do this?" Extensive upper body strengthening would be necessary to be able to do this easily. "It looks so easy, but whoa, . . . it is not!" I struggle and manage to turn the boat around. Rowing backwards feels easier but I can't see where we're going. Frontward rowing is way different from backward rowing. I resolve to work on my upper body. My lower body is strong, from mountain biking and hiking a lot. This is really hard. How embarrassing. The roar of an upcoming rapid grows louder. "Here, Randy. Your turn," and I hand over the oars.

Brooke, Jenn and Mac eddy out. Brooke gives Mac running tips. Next is Russian Rapids, Class II, named after Russian Creek. The surrounding woods are lovely. An osprey flies by out fishing. Off we go.

Russian Rapids. Mac flips. Again I panic and hold my breath till he's out of danger. Again I hold on tight as we run the rapid, thinking only of reaching him. I worry.

"Are you okay?" we greet him.

"Yeah, I just paddled too far to the right, then over compensated, and, *boom,* I was swimming."

I breathe again. Time to reapply sunscreen. Randy got sunburned yesterday. My motherly instincts kick in, "YoMama says, *Wear your sunscreen, Randy. Reapply. Reapply!*" I insist he wear a SPF#30 today.

Loren and Dreux keep their knees covered with the towel.

On down the river we run. The names of rapids amuse me: China Gulch, Washboard, Slim Pickins, Big Windy Chute, Horseshoe Bend, Stair Creek Falls, Blossom Bar, Devil's Stairscase, Brushy Bar. A good guide has lots of stories to go with the names. Sometimes running the rapids, bopping downstream through the countryside, music sings in my head, *Eine Kleine Nachtmusik* by Mozart and Beethoven's *Pastoral* and especially Smetana's *The Moldau.* It feels like a foreign film.

At Upper Black Bar Falls, Class III, Randy puts the run to a vote. "Do you want to run it safe or do you want to take the sport run?"

Refusing to be responsible, "I pass," comes out of my mouth.

"Me too," Loren adds.

"Sport run!" yelps Dreux.

"Oh, wait a minute. Can I change my mind?" trying to renege.

"Too late," Randy knows me pretty well by now, sure that I'm game. "Sport run it is. Watch out for a great big hole."

Brooke, Jenn and Mac run to the right side of middle.

Randy positions us for just left of middle. I hold on tight. We drop over the falls and hit the hole. Dreux, Loren and I get drenched.

"Yeah!" we passengers wail, "Good guiding, Randy."

Up ahead we see Jenn stand up in her boat, put her arms up in the air and make funny motions with her hands. My first thought is of an animal. *She's trying to tell us there's something big and scary close by,* I guess.

"Paddles. Someone lost their paddle. Look out for paddles," Randy commands and we respond by scanning the shoreline and water for lost hardware. We don't find any liberated gear and catch up with Jenn.

"Did you see the bears?" Jenn excitedly greets us.

We have a big discussion about paddles and bears then laugh at ourselves. We missed the bears. We decide not to tell Larry and the family, thinking Beth and Elaine might freak at news of a bear sighting.

The weather today is perfect again. We couldn't have had better weather. Loren jumps into the river to cool off.

"Reapply," YoMama reminds.

Randy pulls the boats over for lunch at a cute little creek, Jenny Creek, running crystal clear water. I am off to find the outhouse.

I wander up the canyon to explore the creek. I toss a dried leaf into the creek's whitewater. The leaf floats over a mini-waterfall and swirls around underwater caught in a hole and pops out downstream. I imagine myself as the leaf if I were tossed out of the boat and how the river would move me through the water. I find another leaf and launch it. Again the leaf drops over the fall, swirls around in the hole and pops out. I find a stick, launch it and notice the same movements flowing downstream. One difference is that a person floating downstream would have on a life jacket that might alter the natural tendency of the flow. Somehow, this play eases my fears of being tossed overboard and being at the river's mercy.

"One, two, three. LUNCH!!" the guides sing. Burrito Buffet. Great lunch.

Before getting back into the water, Brooke takes Mac aside and coaches him concerning the next run, Horseshoe

Bend, Class III. Randy joins in and reiterates avoiding a big hole on the left. I feel a little nervous listening to the precautions.

Randy encourages Mac, "You've got it; you're doing great. Just read the river and run it."

Off we go and I hold on tight.

Horseshoe Bend slopes downhill steeper than any of the previous runs. And since it is a bend, it's not possible to see what's around the corner. The Rogue is full of surprises. I can't imagine running it without a guide. Imagine being the first person to run a river. Who was the first person to run the Rogue? I love rivers.

Down we go. Mac heads left to center. Randy mumbles out loud, "Stay away from the left, Mac. Go right." Mac cruises through easily and disappears left around the bend. "It's washed out. The hole is gone. High water this year," Randy concludes. Horseshoe Bend rolls downhill surrounded by the loveliest woods. We paddle on for another hour or so.

"Where do you hope to camp tonight?" I ask Randy, guessing that he has his favorite spots and is moving us along so we can get to a campsite before someone else takes it.

"Today will be a short day on the water. I'd like to get Kelsey Creek Camp. It's on the left bank and it's great," Randy responds. "There's a beautiful waterfall, Kelsey Falls, upstream. It's a good hike."

It's still early afternoon. We have plenty of daylight left to paddle but I trust Randy.

Brooke and Jenn don't get the message about Kelsey Creek Camp. Randy signals them for the next spot, Battle Bar Camp. "It's the site of a battle between the local Native Americans and some gold rush settlers. The whites wiped out the Indians. There's an old cabin with a plaque." The boats glide gently down the river giving us time to let our imaginations ignite.

"Yes!" Randy exclaims as we round another bend. "It's ours."

Brooke has already beached.

Randy was right. This spot is special. We unload the drybags. Randy leads us on an uphill trail to plenty of private campsites and the historic cabin downstream. Dreux and Loren discover a great spot nestled in some trees. Mac and I find a super spot on a cliff overlooking the river. Perfect, as long as we don't walk in our sleep. Larry and the family claim an area on the other side of the trail upstream. Nearby, we set up the folding chairs on a cliff overlooking the river.

Sooner than we can set up our tent, Brooke and Jenn deliver the hors d'oeuvre table. They are doing a great job of spoiling us.

Mac and I settle into our new home.

Soon we wander over to nibble at the snack table. I giggle, "root beer."

"White sugar," Mac reminds.

"Why don't you eat white sugar?" asks Beth.

"Well . . ." the speech begins, "I didn't stop for health reasons. A while back I was studying will power. Once, during that time, I was meditating and it came to me: *In order to help strengthen your will power I challenge you to stop eating white sugar.* It would be difficult for me to stop for any other reason because I love desserts. I used to work as a dessert chef."

Elaine notes, "I wish we could quit. I know it's not good for us. Was it hard to do?"

"Yes, it was a challenge. And sugar is added to a lot of packaged foods, like ketchup. I especially miss chocolate and root beer."

We nibble and chat some more. Then I wander over to explore the cabin.

It was the site of an 1856 skirmish between the U.S. Cavalry and Rogue Indians. More than 500 troops under Colonel Kelsey occupied the right bank, firing at some 200 Indians, mostly women and children, on the left bank. 20 to 30 Indians died; only one soldier was killed.

— from *Western Whitewater*

The cabin feels cold and weird. I don't much like the feeling I get. I return to the tent, light some incense and pull out my notepad. Mac is off somewhere.

Beth "pitters" up along the trail. She pokes her head into the tent and wriggles her nose, "What's that?"

"Incense."

"What's it for?"

"I like the smell of it. I usually light it when I'm going to meditate."

"What's meditate?"

"Well, . . . I lie down, close my eyes and relax for about a half an hour."

"Oh. Why do you do it?"

"Well, if I stay awake and lie still long enough I see beautiful lights dancing in front of my eyes. It's kind of magical. The lights move around and change."

"Oh. I see that sometimes before I go to sleep. Kind of there's little stars that twinkle?"

"Yes. That's it. I love the lights."

"What are you writing?" Beth continues.

"Notes about the trip."

"Oh." Beth hesitates, then asks, "Are you and Mac married?"

"No." Silence sits between us. I don't say it to her but I'm leery of any contract where the only two ways out of it are death or divorce. Neither option appears attractive.

"Do you sleep in the same tent?" she asks.

"Yes." Poor child, I hope this doesn't mess with her head. "We live together. We have for almost five years."

"Do you have kids?"

"I have three children. My oldest daughter lives in Palm Desert, California. She's twenty-three years old. My son lives in Colorado. He's almost twenty. My twelve-year-old daughter lives with us."

"Is Mac a good dad?"

"He's great."

"Can I call him MacDaddy?"

"MacDaddy? That's funny. You'll have to ask him."

The Q&A session continues and I do the best I can.

I ask, "I saw you alone by the river this morning. Do you like to be alone?" She reminds me of myself when I was a Little One.

"Yeah, sometimes. I don't like to be around *them* so much," she says quietly and gestures toward Michael and Davey.

I sense a soft spot. I have a hint of what her life might be like, "I had four brothers and I know how they were with me. They teased me a lot and hit me and, . . . it was sometimes awful. One brother was always nice, never violent. Do your brothers give you a hard time?"

"Yeah. They hit me. One time they locked me in their room and they wouldn't let me out. They tied me up in a chair. I screamed. They're mean to me. I'd rather play alone."

I feel angry, "Nobody should hit you. Nobody should tie you in a chair. Have you told your mom and dad about all this?"

"Yes, but they don't listen. I tell them and they say, *Oh, Beth. They wouldn't do that. Play nice.*"

I empathize with her situation. I had two older brothers and remember knock down battles, protecting myself and chasing them down the streets with brooms. I learned to survive but it shouldn't have been necessary.

"Nobody should ever hit you. It's wrong. What if strangers locked you in a room and tied you to a chair. They'd be in jail for doing that. It's not right. Don't let them get away with it." She's so young and I don't want her to get into the pattern of allowing herself to be abused.

Larry calls to Beth telling her not to bother me.

"She's fine," I assure Dad.

Mac appears.

"Mac, tell her that it's not appropriate for her brothers to lock her in a room and tie her up to a chair."

Mac blinks his eyes and questions Beth, "They did that to you?"

"Yes."

"Did you tell your mom and dad?"

"Yes, but they didn't do anything."

"Tell them again. Ask them to protect you from your brothers. That's not right," Mac confirms.

"Mac?" Little One asks, "Can I call you MacDaddy?"

Mac laughs.

"Can I?"

"MacDaddy, . . . hmm-m. Sure, you can call me MacDaddy."

How could he resist?

Mac hangs out a little longer then takes his book and sleeping pad out of the sun to find a spot in the shade. The hot sun feels good to me but Mac runs hot and he's been paddling all day. I sat on my butt all day, riding the waves and having fun.

Beth hangs out a little longer and, for some reason, tells me that she can cook fried matzo.

I ask for the recipe and write it down, word-for-word:

Beth Fried Matzo

Take fried matzo. Tiny bit of water. Put an egg in it. Crack the shell. Mix it. If it's not watery enough, add water. Take a frying pan. Put it all in there as much as you can. Turn the stove on. Wait 20 minutes. Or 25 minutes. Salt and pepper. Switch sides. I learned it from my grandmother.

"Have you seen the old cabin over there?" I ask. We walk over. Beth slowly reads the plaque aloud and does an excellent job, considering she's only seven.

"I'm going to go back to the tent and meditate. Would you like to meditate with me?" I ask.

She does. We return to the tent and crawl in. We lay silent for about two or three minutes, then Beth says, "I'm finished. Can I leave?"

I unzip the tent and off she goes.

When I come back to Earth, almost everyone is down by the river. I join them. Loren, Davey, Beth and Mac are upstream, wading in the shallows, splashing around.

"Ellen. Come see the newts!" Beth reaches down and pulls up a dripping, slimy, weird-looking thing. "They feel funny. Don't lick 'em."

I've never seen a newt before.

"Davey's got a whole bunch over there in that hole," Beth points. "We're newt herding."

Beth's enthusiasm pleases me. It seems that Davey and Beth get along better than Michael and Beth.

Dinner smells outrageous.

"One, two, three. DINNER!!" sing the guides.

Lasagna! How can they bake lasagna out here? They did. Vegetarian lasagna. Yes, God is here. Remind me to write a thank you note to the meal planner for this trip. Huge salad, garlic bread. Yes, life is good. There's also a spice cake with cream cheese frosting for dessert but I'll pass on that.

After dinner I help wash the dishes.

"You don't *have* to help," Brooke emphasizes.

"I insist. Unless you don't want help?"

"Oh no, if you insist. We've never had a guest like you who *really* wanted to help with the dishes."

"I love it."

"Okay."

I don't want to take the joy away from them and don't want to impose. Cooking and dishes are times when the guides can be alone with each other and talk guide talk. *Is Randy trying to put the move on Brooke? Is Jenn interested in him? Is my imagination too active?* The dishwashing conversations are different from the all-around-the-campfire conversations and I don't want to inhibit anyone. But they let me in.

"I'll tell you what," I have a thought. "I love it here on the Rogue. I'll leave my tent set up here and when you bring guests down the river, I'll come down and help with dinner and the dishes and you can feed me. Okay?" I could live out here all summer. It's a great idea but they don't take me seriously. I'd do it if I could.

After dishes I join Mac, Dreux and Loren up the hill in the patio with a view. Dreux is almost finished with his book. Mac pulls out a cigar, a *Griffin*. We chitchat and ask each other more questions and tell stories. Mac offers his cigar to me. I like to puff on them, occasionally.

Loren's eyes get big.

I puff.

He has to ask, "You smoke cigars?"

"Yeah, you want a puff?" I offer.

"No way. I don't smoke," he retorts.

"Neither do I," I spit back. "You don't inhale. Just draw it into your mouth and blow it out."

"Really?" Loren looks to Mac for confirmation.

"Dreux? You want a puff," trying to corrupt the teenagers on the trip.

"*Griffin.* That's our school mascot," Loren contributes.

Randy climbs the hill and joins us.

We talk about parties. We talk about life. Mac hears about Dreux and Loren's parents sending them on this trip because Mom and Dad were going to the Caribbean for Mom's birthday.

"Where are you going after this?" Mac asks.

"I don't know. The itinerary is in the Volvo. We've got reservations at a bed and breakfast somewhere by Crater Lake." Dreux is definitely in charge.

"Hey, MacDaddy," Beth joins us.

"MacDaddy, I like that," Randy picks up on it. Jenn and Brooke join us too.

"Hey! That's my favorite book of all time," Jenn says to Dreux, regarding *Their Eyes Were Watching God.*

We talk outdoor patio rafting talk and watch the daylight fade.

As the sun sets we wander off to our tents. One thing about the rafting guides that I've encountered is that they haven't used lanterns to stay up late. When it gets dark, we can sit around the fire, talk and sing, or go to bed. Mac gives a new *Griffin* cigar to Loren. "Here, take it to school and insist they let you smoke it because it's your school mascot."

"Yeah, right."

I stay out last and watch the night unfold, hoping to see some falling stars. Randy, Jenn, and Brooke sleep down by the river. They just roll out their tarp, their sleeping bags and sleep. Tonight I hear them whisper. They work all day. They're up first, row those heavy oars most of the day, cook breakfast, lunch and dinner, clean up and watch out for us. They put in a long day. I turn in.

June 23, Friday ☽ ♉
The Rogue River, Day Three

Courage is the resistance to fear, the mastery of fear, . . . not the absence of fear.

— Mark Twain

What is that noise? I hop up and unzip the tent. Geese. Across the river sit half a dozen Canada geese greeting the day. I thank them for waking me up. I pull on warm clothes and quietly settle down to watch the day begin. Deer, . . . and a crane, I think. It flies with its neck out front, feet out back and no visible topnotch.

I love morning time. It's so quiet and the light is unlike the light at any other time of the day. The guides aren't up yet. I meditate.

Pancakes and fruit for breakfast. The kids adopt MacDaddy as their big buddy. Drybags have to be ready to load by 9 a.m.

It's off down the river we go. Before too long we stop and tie up the boats on the north shore. Zane Grey's cabin. It's an easy hike up the hill. At the trail's end sits the original log cabin, preserved for tourists, with a caretaker's house close by. Behind the cabin spreads a large grassy area big enough to double as an emergency heliopad. The sprinkler is on. I run through it before anybody can tell me not to. Michael and Davey run after me, get yelled at and stop. A friendly cat finds Beth. Up on the hillside, the vegetable garden feels inviting but is surrounded in a seven-foot tall wire electrical fence, probably to keep the deer out. The caretaker's house has some impressively old rose bushes. Randy directs our attention to a small garden of rocks piled underneath a sprawling shade tree.

"What do each of those rocks have in common?" our head guide quizzes.

I look but nothing immediately comes to mind. Then I notice that each rock is shaped like a heart. Others don't see it as quickly but eventually someone blurts out, *hearts*. I could stay here all day. I could live here. It is gorgeous. But head guide hurries us back to the boats.

"We've got a long day ahead of us," Randy warns. "We've got the Rogue River Ranch, Mule Creek Canyon, Blossom Bar Rapid, Devil's Staircase and I hope to camp at Brushy Bar Creek."

It all sounds fun to me. Mule Creek Canyon and Blossom Bar will be the last of our Class IV rapids. After Blossom Bar, the river tames. In fact it gets so tame that, . . .

In the summer big jet boats ply the river above Grave Creek and below Blossom Bar, whisking sightseers down from Grants Pass or up from the coast.
— from *Western Whitewater*

Back in the boats, we bop downstream for another hour or so. The runs are fun and we get plenty wet. "Reapply," YoMama commands. Mac runs the rapids like a pro. I feel excited to see an adult river otter with two babies. This is my first time ever seeing river otters.

It seems too early to stop for lunch but we do. Time just flies when you're having fun. We stop at one of the most visited tourist stops along the river, The Rogue River Ranch. Brooke pulls out the GORP. Beth takes my hand and up a trail we go. At the top we find a huge grassy area that's big enough for a football game. A tractor is busy mowing. Off at the other end of the field is a brightly painted farm compound, . . . red. I'm sure it could be easily spotted from the air. I feel like I'm coming home.

On the river side of the property is a grand garden, surrounded in seven-foot wire fencing, featuring rows of veggies and herbs. I am home. An older lady is planting flowers next to one of the big, red buildings.

"Are you the gardener?" I ask.

"Yes. I'm one of them."

"Do you live here all year 'round?"

"No, just for the season. We leave in the winter."

Thinking to my future, I ask, "How can I get your job?"

"We're all volunteers. We get a room and a food allotment."

She looks well fed and happy. Perfect. I'd volunteer to work here for at least one summer. I'll bet there's a waiting list or you have to know someone who knows someone. Maybe I'll write a letter now to let them know I'll be ready in about seven or eight years when Aja is older. This is heaven. I say that everywhere I land but I really feel it.

We wander around the ranch, finding a little museum in the original log cabin. It gives a feel of what it might have been like a century ago. We explore a tack room/barn. Yes, I could stay here for a while.

Back at the beach, lunch is excellent as usual with sandwiches and a pasta salad. Weather today is very hot. A man and a woman sit on a blanket in a *primo* shade spot close by on the beach. They invite us over so we can get out of the sun. Mac, Loren and I take them up on it. The man used to be a guide years ago on the Rogue. He and his girlfriend are taking a week and going down the river alone in their own boat. Oh how wonderful. They're camped up above in a field. A solar shower stretches out on the sand, filled with water, absorbing heat.

"Does it work?" I ask, missing a hot shower.

"Yes!" The woman answers quickly. "We wouldn't leave home without it."

After lunch, we load up, thank the couple for their hospitality, wish them well and go on our merry way. Mule Creek Canyon is the next adventure. We eddy out to discuss the run before entering.

"Okay, MacDaddy, you know what to do," Randy shows confidence in Mac's newly learned river running abilities. "The river squeezes through a narrow passage creating a lot of turbulence and boils. The river can move a boat anywhere it wants. Pay attention. In one spot the canyon narrows to only ten feet wide. Watch your paddle. At the end, keep an eye open for Coffee Pot, the mother of all boils. You can do it Mac. Read and run. No flipping here, okay MacDaddy?"

"Flipdaddy!" someone invents.

I silently pray for his safe passage. I'm glad I'm not paddling so I can keep an eye on him. He'll do fine.

Living life as a human spirit on Earth is like running a river. You can go through life trusting the guides and in doing so learn to trust yourself. If you choose, you can practice and learn to run the river alone or even become a guide. But the river is never the same river twice. The water is never the same water. The water levels vary. The weather is always a factor. The guests change. The river of life is a great adventure. Hone the skills, prepare for what's around the next bend, then tackle it. Be aware of challenges and opportunities. Relax. Have fun. Sometimes fear rears its ugly head. Use the fear. Love the fear. Evolve it into concern, caution, respect and awareness. Become good. Enjoy the ride. Learn to read the river and then run it. Then at the end of the day stand at the river's edge and howl at the silver moon that shines down from above.

Mac disappears downstream into Mule Creek Canyon. This stretch was used in the movie, *The River Wild*, with Meryl Streep. The river narrows. The canyon walls close in and close out the view. It's like a winding tunnel with no top.

I can't see Mac and feel nervous. What if he flips and gets caught in these boils? What if? We bounce around a little. I can't imagine doing this in an inflatable ducky. This big oar boat feels safe.

Leaving Mule Creek Canyon, Randy points out Coffee Pot, a boil, gurgling with turbulence. Mac sits up ahead safe in his boat.

"Hey, Flipdaddy," I yell.

He pats the top of his helmet signaling that he's okay.
It's good to see you! Thank you, Universe.

He smiles. I'm so proud of him. It took a lot of courage to do what he's done the last three days.

It's mellow rafting now, Randy lets me row for a while. It's a struggle but I thoroughly enjoy rowing. When I hear a rapid downstream, I hand over the oars. Randy runs the next rapids effortlessly like a pro. Hey, . . . he is a pro.

Blossom Bar. Now I see why they call it Blossom Bar. The surrounding hillsides are blooming with colorful, wild azaleas. It's too beautiful. We tie up the boats on the north shore. Blossom Bar, Class IV, is a mandatory scout. Mac has read about this rapid in his books and magazines. Blossom Bar.

Head guide makes sure everyone keeps on their life jackets as we scurry up to the lookout. *Western Whitewater* describes this run as "a long, technical boulder garden." It is. Randy discusses the run with Brooke and Jenn. Randy thinks it is far too dangerous for Mac and the ducky to run. I don't want to go down it in the big boat, let alone watch Mac go down in the ducky.

We find a rock to sit and read the flow.

Suddenly we see Randy going down Blossom Bar in Mac's ducky. Randy executes the rapid successfully and quickly pulls over to the north shore just downstream from us. He ties up the ducky and walks up the hill toward us. Emotion fills Mac's face.

"I wanted to run it," Mac expresses.

"In the ducky?" I ask.

"If not in the ducky, I want to at least run it in the oar boat." Mac has looked forward to this rapid the entire trip.

Randy climbs to the lookout. "Okay, Flipdaddy. There's your ducky."

More disappointment wells up on Mac's face. "I want to run Blossom Bar," he informs Randy.

"In the ducky? It's too dangerous," Randy answers.

"How about in the oar boat?" Mac offers.

"Yes, we could make room." Randy looks puzzled then says, "But I thought, ..."

I sense tension.

Randy and Mac discuss the issue briefly then decide to deflate the ducky and put it in the oar boat. The oar boat wouldn't be able to pull over so quickly after running Blossom Bar to let Mac pick up his ducky. Randy and Mac head downstream toward the ducky. I head back upstream to the oar boat.

Wait, I could take the ducky downstream from here and Mac could ride Blossom Bar in the oar boat. That way, Mac gets what he wants and I don't have to go down Blossom Bar. I backtrack up to the lookout but Randy and Mac are already heading my direction with the deflated ducky.

We meet back up at the lookout. Brooke's boat, with all the family sitting up front, takes off. We watch. She enters the rapid.

Randy watches then jumps up and yells, "Get to the center. Get to the center!"

Brooke's boat drops the fall, bumps a boulder and instantly Beth and Elaine roll out of the boat into the waves.

"Oh my God," I pray and watch for Beth's brightly-colored life jacket and helmet between the waves. The waves are huge and she disappears for long periods of time. Swimmers float faster than boats in whitewater and off they go, bobbing up and down in the water, barely missing partially submerged boulders. Downstream waits a huge eddy on the left. They'll go there. I fear for them and say another prayer.

We scurry down the hill. Randy leaves us in the dust. Mac and I take a wrong turn and lose the trail. Soon we realize it and find our way back down to the boat.

When we reach the boat Randy has finished tying in the ducky and snaps at us, "We have people in the water, folks. Let's move it!"

Jenn is already gone chasing Brooke's boat and looking for swimmers.

Dreux, Loren, Mac and I squeeze into the front of the boat. I show Mac where to hold on. Worrying about Beth and Elaine in the water partly takes my mind off running Blossom Bar but not entirely. I'm nervous. Mac is on the outside and I don't want him to fall out. Off we go.

Blossom Bar is such a pretty name for such a scary rapid. We miss some boulders and lightly touch the one that dumped Beth and Elaine. I grab onto Mac. We bounce and bump but make it through. My eyes are fixed downstream looking for the signal that everything is okay. I don't see it. We pass the quiet eddy on the left. Nobody. Devil's Staircase, the next rapid. Where are they?

"There they are!" Randy yells. Beyond Devil's Staircase, sitting in a calm, both boats have eddied out with Elaine and a shivering Beth aboard. I breathe a heavy sigh and we tackle Devil's Staircase.

Not bad, if you stay away from the right wall. We descend the bumpy run. *Did they swim this? Oh my God. It's a washboard.* We catch up to them and Elaine sits silent and shivering. Beth is crying hysterically. It's so good to see them both alive.

"Are you okay?" I ask.

Neither says a word.

I sigh again and give thanks.

The wind picks up. A huge tourist jet boat obligingly slows down when it sees us. It seems rather obscene and feels like an intrusion on our wilderness river ride. *Jet boats, which can ascend the river to the foot of Blossom Bar, may be seen at any time,* (from *Western Whitewater*). I feel a quiet energy from all three of our boats and wonder how Brooke is taking this. I wonder if she is thinking that the Blossom Bar incident was her fault? I wonder if Randy thinks it could have been handled differently. I wonder why these stupid tourists don't just stay off our river and take their loud, polluting, gas-guzzling crafts somewhere else. I wonder a lot. And I hope. I hope Elaine and Beth won't be traumatized and that this doesn't ruin the trip for them. The wind blows up the river relentlessly in our faces.

Brushy Bar camp is occupied. Randy heads for Solitude Bar. We float in silence.

It's ours. We unload the drybags. The mood is somber. I ask each family member if she/he is okay and check in with Brooke. Mac and I find a great tent site and offer it to Larry. Larry takes it. He guides his family and their belongings up the hill and sets up their tents. Elaine and Beth disappear. I'm sure the ladies are happy to be warm and on dry ground.

Randy, Brooke and Jenn engage in emotional conversation while they unload the boats and set up the kitchen. I see many hugs and a few tears. I walk over to them. Mac follows me. We embrace for a group hug.

Dreux and Loren look like they're trying to fly a kite rather than set up a tent. It's almost comical. Eventually the wind wins the wrestling match. Loren and Dreux abandon the tent, piled in a heap.

After Mac and I set up our tent, I run off to find the outhouse. One little trail leads to another. The woods are enchanting, knee-high with wood sorrel, ferns and flowers. This is the first time we've camped on the north shore and this must be the 37-mile trail that follows the river. I'd love to hike this trail.

The toilet is a little further from camp than we're used to, quite a way downstream but the walk through the woods is gorgeous. I keep my eyes open for lions, tigers and bears.

When I'm finished with my business I run back to camp. "Mac. Have you seen the woods up there? Come on, it's fantastic." Reluctantly, he follows me. We walk around and explore. We're up the hill from camp, hidden from view.

Mac looks at me with concern, "Do you think that was my fault at Blossom Bar? I mean, if I hadn't insisted on riding the rapid in the oar boat, Randy wouldn't have had to go back to get the ducky, and . . . ."

"Oh no, Sweetheart. That was not your fault." I can't believe that Mac is blaming himself for what happened. "I'm sure that everyone down there thinks it was his or her fault that it happened. Brooke feels bad. I'm sure she's replaying in her mind whether or not she could have prevented it. Brooke ran Blossom Bar like every other rapid we've run the last three days. Elaine probably feels it's her fault Beth rolled out of the boat. Larry probably thinks he could have held on tighter or grabbed onto them as they rolled out into the water. Randy, . . . he's the head guide; he feels everything is his responsibility. Even Jenn might think she could have been more help. Don't put this on yourself.

"For whatever reason, and there may not even be a reason, Elaine and Beth rolled out of the boat and swam those rapids. Their family is a self-perpetuating microcosm. Who knows what's going on inside of the family dynamics to have created such a scenario. It wasn't your fault. Don't do that to yourself. Let's just be thankful everyone is okay."

We walk a bit in the woods then head back down to camp.

The hors d'oeuvre table is ready on schedule. Randy announces, "Tonight the juice thermos is off limits to the kids. Night Three is traditionally Margarita Night on the trip and the small thermos is full of a lethal tequila concoction. So kids, leave this one alone. Sodas are in the blue cooler. Okay?"

Somehow it doesn't feel much like a celebration. It was a rough afternoon. Elaine and Beth still haven't made an appearance. I suspect they're napping. I've got kind of a stress headache, so I seek refuge in our tent. Beth walks up the path emerging from the family compound.

"Hi, Beth. How are you doing?" How many times daily do we say those words and not really mean them? I eagerly wait for her response. An experience like Beth just had at her age could mess her up for the rest of this life and maybe into the next. "What are you feeling?"

She doesn't want to talk.

"Would you like to meditate with me?"

"Sure."

"Tell your mom and dad where you'll be so they don't worry."

She does, returns and off we go to the tent. I light some incense, *Morning Star*. Rose is my favorite scent. Each box comes with a small square tile that has a hole in it to hold the incense. I place it on my pocket mirror to stabilize it and keep it away from the nylon tent floor. Beth seems fascinated.

"Where do you get the incense?"

"The Sunrise Grocery, a Japanese market in Monterey. I'll tell you what, when our river trip is finished, I'll give you all of the incense I have left and the tile. Would you like that?" I hope this helps to cheer her up.

"Really?"

"You'll have to ask your mom or dad to light it for you, okay?"

"Great," and she seems to brighten up a little and lays down on Mac's sleeping bag.

"If you start seeing those twinkling lights, watch them, enjoy them. They're so beautiful," my last-minute tip.

"Like the lights I see before I go to sleep?"

"That's them." I lay down and we go quiet. Beth shuffles to get comfortable. I hear the Rogue roaring, the wind blowing and the guides talking. I slip away.

I come back. Beth is so quiet that I'm sure she's fallen asleep. I sit up. She sits up.

She smiles, "I feel better."

I smile back, "Me too."

We leave the tent. Mac, Loren, Davey and Michael have started up a ballgame, of sorts. They're using a stick for the bat and a knotted up sock for the ball. Beth joins the festivities. I'm glad to see she's getting back to her happy self. They play for a while and I offer my help in the kitchen.

We talk about the near catastrophe and I try to reassure Brooke that it wasn't her fault. She still feels bad.

"Did you see Larry when Elaine and Beth went over?" Brooke reports.

Randy becomes animated. "Larry was hanging over the side of the boat taking pictures of them with his waterproof camera! He said 'I wish I had brought the video camera.' I couldn't believe it."

Mac, Dreux, and Loren have already been into the margarita jug. I haven't been drinking alcohol for the last two years but today might be a good day to indulge. We'll call it a celebration that Elaine and Beth are physically okay.

"Is there sugar in the margarita mix?" I ask the guides. We go through the trash and confirm the inclusion of sugar in the mix contents. I turn my attention to the half-full bottle of tequila. "Can I sip from there?" pointing to the bottle of tequila, finding some boldness within.

"By all means, YoMama! Here, I'll join you," Randy sings. We take our plastic *Echo* mugs and Randy extends his talents to bartender. We toast, clink and down a hit. My body chills and shivers all the way through. It's been a long time. I haven't missed alcohol too much. Socially, I've become comfortable abstaining in bars or at parties. I don't miss the hangovers at all.

The ballgame ends. I stick out my mug for another hit. Randy sees that I'm in a sporting mood and pours. Randy turns to Mac, "Hey, FlipDaddy, want a swig?" Dreux and Loren hit the thermos jug.

It doesn't take much for me to get silly and soon all the guys are making fun of me. I don't care. I'm making fun of me too.

Eventually, the discussion returns to the day's event at Blossom Bar. "Did you know that Larry had a disposable waterproof camera and was taking pictures of Elaine and Beth in the water?" I ask Mac and the boys.

"You are kidding," they send back.

It's good to hear that I'm not the only one who thinks that strange behavior.

"Remember what Davey said the first night at Doe Bar?" Loren speaks up.

"No, what?" I ask.

"Remember when he said, 'I wish my mom would fall overboard and drown.' Remember?" Loren is serious.

"No." Then I recall Davey the Fire Master. "No, I didn't hear that." I wonder what Davey is feeling about all of this now?

We chitchat and get silly.

Up on the hill Dreux and Loren's tent sits piled in a heap, the wind tossing it about. I have to ask, "What about your tent?"

Dreux unscrupulously tosses a playful growl, "Forget the *freakin'* tent."

Using the "F" word is so out of character for Dreux that we all laugh at his sudden lack of concern.

"Where are you going to sleep tonight?" I ask.

"Forget the *freakin'* tent," he growls again a little louder, tipping back in his beach chair. "I don't care. I'll sleep right here." The tequila has slipped Dreux into a different gear.

"Come on. Mac and I will help you," I offer. "I might know what the problem is."

Mac and Loren follow me to the synthetic heap.

"Come on, Dreux," I coax.

He does.

My mothering instincts kick in. "First of all we've got to unzip the door *and* the window. The wind is blowing into the tent and creating a parachute effect."

The boys hold up the tent while I crawl inside and begin to execute the plan.

"Next we've got to anchor it." I go to look for the right rocks. I find a good-sized one and position it in the right front corner facing the wind.

Loren does the same for the left corner.

We throw in the sleeping bags to help keep the tent down.

Dreux watches.

"There you go! It's up." I'm glad it worked.

We leave the boys to set up house. Mac and I wander back to camp. There's still plenty of daylight. Michael is off playing alone. Larry and Davey are munching snacks.

"Are they okay?" I ask Larry, referring to the ladies.

"Elaine didn't want to come on this trip anyway. But she'll be fine. She just needs to rest. They'll be just fine. They're just a bit shaken up," Larry passes on.

Larry's seemingly lack of concern bothers me. My first thought would have been to help those in the water. "I heard you were taking pictures while they were in the water?"

"Yeah, it was great!" Larry starts. "Don't tell Elaine, though. I don't think she'll appreciate it just yet. I'll wait till I get the pictures. Elaine grabbed onto Beth immediately but lost hold. While in the water, Beth saw Brooke pointing to the eddy on the left and started swimming toward it but Elaine didn't see it. Beth had to decide whether to go to the eddy or to her mom. She went to her mom. She could hardly swim any more. They were cold and exhausted. When we caught up to them at the top of Devil's Staircase, I grabbed Beth and pulled her into the boat. We couldn't get Elaine till after the rapid."

Great ideas originate in the muscles.

— Thomas A. Edison

I wander off to see the sights and be alone. It feels good to be on a trail in the woods *and* a bit tipsy.

A large boulder stands alone on the sandbar. I climb up. I'm glad we didn't camp here. The kids would be climbing all over this and I'd be a nervous wreck worrying about them falling off. If I were a kid this'd be where I'd play. Solitude Riffle bends around the rocks and curves to the north. I feel Native American energy again. If I were a Tutuni or Takelma this would have been a great place to spend the summer. My guess is that there used to be plenty of fish and game here. This feels like a special spot.

I climb back up the hill and meet the trail, then continue walking downstream away from camp. All of a sudden I start running and it feels good.

A dream I once had comes to mind. Even though I had the dream over ten years ago it's still so real and intense. I was a deer and had a deer family. The deer would all meet in the meadow when the moon was full and celebrate with the moondance. I remember being at peace, happy and full of love. The Earth was a glorious place filled with joy. The dream covered many seasons. I was a deer for a long time. Then one day as I was wandering through the woods nibbling on leaves and berries, . . . BOOM!!! I jumped and ran to escape the loud sound. And I ran. I was so frightened. Soon I met up with some deer friends and described what I had heard. They told me that it was called *man* and something else called *gunshot*. Time moved on. We always met and moondanced in the meadow at full moon. I was content and happy. Life was good. Then one day, again while grazing, another BOOM broke the silence. *Man!* I jumped and ran and ran and ran. I was so frightened that time began moving slowly. Another *gunshot* sounded. Then another. While running I heard a very clear voice exclaim, "You have the choice: Deer or *man*. The choice is yours." I remember not knowing what to do. I loved being a deer. *Man* seemed to be very powerful but frightening. I ran, feeling desperate, confused and full of fear. Then I woke up. I sat up wide-awake, surprised to see that I was a human. What happened? I felt homesick and sad. Waking up was like leaving home.

Running through these woods along the Rogue reminds me of being a deer. I miss the woods. I miss the other deer and the meadows in the moonlight. *Man* is powerful, yes, but maybe doesn't know how to use the power or, conversely, chooses to abuse it. *Man* can be self-centered and out of touch with the universal bigger picture. I've seen another way to live on Earth and it is good. *Man*, (and I include myself), has a lot to learn from this planet's other inhabitants.

Beth comes to mind. I've been afraid this whole river run of falling out of the boat and swimming the rapids, especially the notorious Blossom Bar. And she did it. Beth did it and survived. I turn around and run back toward camp.

Beth is sitting next to her dad. I try to tell her what's in my heart: "Most adults fear what you did today. *I'm* afraid of it. You may have just done the scariest thing of your whole life. Imagine having that over and done with when you're seven years old? You may have experienced the worst thing that could possibly happen to you in this lifetime — falling off a boat with your mother into whitewater and trying desperately to get to her. Amusement park rides can't hold a candle to the ride you had at Blossom Bar on the Rogue River. It was real. I'll bet your brothers are kind of jealous because you swam Blossom Bar, Class IV. Now they probably wish they had fallen out. You can go back to school and tell everyone of your great adventure. I'm so proud of you, Beth." I hope I make some sense.

"One, two, three, DINNER!!" the guides sing. Dinner looks great. Chicken *fajitas*. I pass on the meat and have a *fajita* salad. Elaine joins us for dinner. Beth starts to talk about her adventure and gets a lot of attention. Soon the boys look full of envy. Elaine seems to be fine. She's smiling.

Brownies for dessert, baked in an iron Dutch oven nestled in hot coals, helps to cheer up everybody.

After dessert Randy asks us to remain seated for the awards ceremony. He fetches a cardboard box and sets it next to his chair. From a sheet of paper he reads the accolades. He starts with the youngest, Beth. He applauds her courage and presents her with an *Echo* T-shirt.

We applaud.

Then one-by-one Randy says a kind word about each of us and presents T-shirts. He ends with Mac, MacDaddy, FlipDaddy, the Flip Master, the Duck *Meister*.

Then we give special mention to the guides. We all sit around and talk for a while and watch the sun set. Elaine and Beth excuse themselves. Soon, the whole family disappears.

We finish off the tequila and watch the sky turn colors then fade to black.

"You know what I found out?" Randy pops in. "Going into Blossom Bar, the entire family had lost their fear of the river. They figured the trip had been accident-free up till that point and Blossom Bar would be a cakewalk. They compared it to a carnival ride — fun without caution. Not one of them held onto the boat. All five of them were holding onto each other."

Going through the rapids I usually hold on to the boat as tightly as I can. Randy's explanation helps me see how the incident happened. It makes more sense. It's been a long day and we all turn in early.

June 24, Saturday ☽ ♉
The Rogue River, Day Four

As on any commercial river trip, the boatmen — and often, these days the boatwomen — are the best part of the trip. The most interesting part. The rest is scenery.

— Edward Abbey, *Down the River*

The sunrise is special. A deer nibbles on the grass in the field close by. The wind has stopped and it's another beautiful day. We have truly been blessed with perfect weather on this trip. Today is our last day. We should get to take-out after lunch. I don't want it to end and retreat back into the tent to meditate.

Everyone gets to sleep in late today. Drybags don't have to be ready until 10 a.m. I take a walk before breakfast.

We load up and paddle on. Beth is reluctant but then courageously climbs aboard and it looks as if all is forgiven. Her tears have dried. It's nice to see a smile on her face.

The tourist jet boats interrupt the morning calm. They're required by law to slow down whenever they see a non-motorized boat. We probably irritate them as much as they irritate us.

We pass the men's group from Galice. They're camped at a fun beach on the north shore. They have giant squirt tubes and try to spray us with water as we float by. Men will be boys.

The Rogue calms down quite a bit on this last stretch. Randy looks for waves to splash us with. It seems no matter which side Dreux sits on he gets the wettest. I accuse Randy of aiming the boat to optimize maximum splashing of Dreux. Randy demonstrates his abilities and heads the boat into oncoming waves and I get soaked.

"Reapply, YoMama, reapply," the boys sing.

We hit a calm spot. Randy asks if I want to take over the oars while he takes a dip.

"Sure." I climb up to the seat. The soreness in my arms reminds me that I did this yesterday. It looks so easy when the guides do it but I struggle. Randy climbs back in the boat. I hear a rapid coming up and resign my post.

"Nope, you do it," Randy says.

"No way. I don't do rapids." I look ahead. An osprey dips in front of us, catches a fish, and circles overhead.

"There's nothing to hit here. You can do it. Read and run, YoMama." Randy encourages.

I stand up and once again offer him the seat but he doesn't move.

"Nope, you're going to do it. You'll do fine," the head guide sounds more confident than I feel.

On the north shore a Great Blue Heron stands on a rock, looks our way and flies off upstream. *That's a sign. I can do it,* I hear from inside of me.

I position the boat in the center of the tongue and go. At first I try to push and fight, then I learn to ride the waves and let the river guide me. I use the oars sparingly to make subtle turns. My arms feel like they're going to give out. Just as I get the hang of it, the riffle ends. "I did it!"

"Yea, YoMama!" the passengers congratulate.

I resolve to work on my upper body strength.

Loren takes the next run. He does a great job and we all delight in his success. He also does a fine job of splashing Dreux, Randy and me.

"Reapply," we chime.

Lunch comes early. Randy wants to show us some *really cool waterfalls*. We beach at a great spot with a nifty swimming hole. The day is hot and the cold water feels quite refreshing. Randy leads a walking tour up to the waterfalls. Brooke and Jenn fix lunch. Mac grabs his camera and we wander off.

The group passes the first waterfall. Mac and I stop and stay. I climb into the chilly pool and Mac gets the camera. My huge red shorts balloon up in the cold water. It seems like it takes forever to snap a picture and it's hard to keep a smile on my face.

We find the trail leading up to the second waterfall, Flora Dell Falls, where we find Randy and the group. A natural dam borders the pool front and a walkway hides behind the fall. We enter into the middle of an emotional display. Michael is screaming at the top of his lungs at his parents. He's balancing on the dam and going ballistic. I look to Dreux, Randy and Loren for an explanation but they shrug their shoulders indicating they don't have a clue. Michael flips out. Larry starts giving him commands. Davey swims across the pool. Michael loses control again. I wonder what's going on but glad that I'm not involved. The family microcosm hit a bump.

The group clears out and heads downhill for lunch. I climb into the little pool again and Mac takes more pictures. If my shorts had elastic on the bottom, they could be used as a flotation device. The water is cold but this is paradise. It'd be so much fun to run the Rogue and take time, say about a month, getting to know all the little side creeks, canyons, waterfalls and everything.

Bagel sandwiches for lunch. Nummy. Elaine and Beth are fine. They say they'd raft again someday.

As soon as we board for launch, a water fight breaks out. Randy and Jenn soak each other.

The river flattens from here to take-out at Foster Bar Landing, nothing but riffles. We take it slowly knowing the end is near.

"I can see it now," Randy thinks out loud, "when I guide my next paddle trip, I have a new command. It'll go, *forward paddle, back paddle, right back, left back, stop, reapply, reapply.*"

It's been such a fun trip, thinking back to the first morning at Galice. *Thank you, River, for our safe journey. Thank you, Universe, for all the guidance and love. Thank you, God, for the beautiful countryside and the river. Thank you, Randy, for being such a stellar guide. Thank you, Dreux and Loren, for being such great company. Thank you, Mac, for this great adventure.* Thanks all around. I'd do it again in a minute.

Down the river we see our first electrical wire stretching above and across the river. Civilization. We're back. Darn. Then we see take-out. Folks, boats, shuttle vans, cars. It's over. We glide into shore and find a spot amongst the crowd. Where did all of these people come from?

We unload the drybags. I find mine, dig inside and get my travel bag. I walk over to Beth and give her the incense and the little blue tile. She smiles and gives me a big hug.

Our shuttle isn't here yet. Larry had paid someone to drive their van here so they could make a fast getaway. Larry is the only one with any cash, so he tips the guides for all of us. Dreux and Mac take Larry's address to send reimbursement. Whatever they tip the guides, I don't think it is enough. Those kids worked their butts off and their work is not finished. They have to completely unload, dismantle, deflate and pack up the boats. We say good-bye to Larry, Elaine and the Little Ones, with hugs all around.

We help the guides unload. Mac takes a picture of all the gear piled in a heap with the guides crashed out on top. Great picture.

Our shuttle arrives. We grab a couple of beers for the long winding ride back to Galice. The guides have to wait for their shuttle truck. We say our good-byes to Randy, Brooke and Jenn and make plans to meet for dinner in Grants Pass.

The ride back is fun but it feels strange to be in a wheeled vehicle. I like the river better. The roadside scenery is beautiful with the Rogue flowing below us. The driver tells us some local stories. We reminisce. Dreux's birthday is May 24th, the day before Mac's. Loren's birthday is March 6th, three days before mine. No wonder we all get along so well.

When we arrive at Galice, we're delighted to see our cars still here in one piece. We unload and confirm plans for the evening. We postpone good-byes until later. Dreux and Loren go on their merry way.

How strange it feels to be back in our car.

We buy some chips and beer, drive to Grants Pass and find a motel. There's nothing like a hot shower after four days without one. Mac spreads out on the king-size bed and falls asleep.

I can't stay indoors so out I go. The motel is on the Rogue riverbank, the upper Rogue — the urban Rogue. The motel is one of the largest in town and offers jet boat rides on the river. Obscene. The pollution is obvious.

We find the designated Thai restaurant that the guides recommended. No one is here yet. No Dreux or Loren. No Randy, Jenn, or Brooke. We wonder if something came up. Dreux said they might have to check into their hotel at Crater Lake before a certain time. Maybe it didn't work out. Maybe the guides got back to the guide house and crashed from exhaustion. We think positively and get a table for seven.

We sit for a while and check out the menu. Mm-m-m, Thai food.

Dreux and Loren pop in. Soon after them, the guides appear. We have a fine dinner and a grand time, laughing and telling stories. Head Guide Randy makes a request that we each take a turn telling our life story in a nutshell.

We exchange addresses and phone numbers. Randy and Brooke live the furthest away. Jenn lives in Santa Cruz, across Monterey Bay.

We all hug and bid *adieu.*

"Good-bye, YoMama. Thanks for trusting me," Randy smiles.

"Thank *you* for everything," I give back. "You are awesome! I want your job."

Randy gives Mac a big hug, "You were great, FlipDaddy. Thanks for the fun time."

Ah, parting is such sweet sorrow. The dream ends.

June 25, Sunday ○ ♊
The Rogue River, Day Five

All paths lead nowhere, so it is important to choose one with heart.
— Carlos Castenada

On the way home, Mac drives up Mount Shasta as far as the road will take us. Above lay beautiful, cold, wet snow. Backpackers, mountaineers, snowboarders, skiers, intrusive snowmobiles, and children play everywhere. The air temperature is 75° – 80°, elevation 6860 feet. I wear shorts, a sports bra and sandals. Here we are beamed instantly from the sweltering summer heat of the flatlands below, up to the dripping ice; done as easily as driving up a mountain road. I read the Carlos Castenada quote on the park sign at the end of the road at Bunny Flat, . . . *it is important to choose one with heart.* I get a body chill, look into my heart and see this book.

We are just passing through the Shasta area. I would love to stay and explore more of it but we are on our way home. If I were twenty years younger I'd want to be a river guide.

PART II — *Get Outta Town*

June 30, Friday ☼ ♋ / ○ Leo ♌
Backpacking 101

Whatever you can do or dream you can, begin it.
— Johann Wolfgang Goethe

Dinkey Lakes Wilderness in the California Sierra Nevada Mountains is to be my first backpacking trip. I have car camped before but never backpacked. How will it be with no cars or phones? How will it be carrying a heavy pack for hours and days? Can I carry enough to be comfortable and warm? What about bears and other critters? What about extreme weather? I am eager to learn. I am eager to go.

Mac is teaching me how to backpack, how to load a pack and what to bring. To prepare for the trip, I practice. My backpack is a hand-me-down, an old Coleman® external frame pack with two main compartments and five outside pockets. I "practice pack" by loading up my pack and walking in my neighborhood looking for challenging hills here on the Monterey Peninsula, California.

Mac and I didn't hike or camp the first five years that we dated. Then he went backpacking with a friend of his and my lower lip drooped, "What about me?"

"I didn't think you liked camping," he said.

"I didn't think *you* liked camping," I responded. We hadn't thought to ask the other. We had never talked about it. We never went hiking.

Then we went car camping to see how I'd do *out there* away from home and the city life. I felt quite at home in the woods and under the starry sky. It seemed to bring back a long-lost memory and filled me with joy. Mac saw that I'm quite comfortable out in the wilds. In fact I'm more comfortable out there than I am anywhere. We went for a long hike and I absolutely loved it. I was so happy to be *out there*.

Over this year we've been collecting equipment: tents, backpacks, sleeping bags, stoves, water filter, etc.

I "practice pack" whenever time allows in preparation for my wilderness backpacking debut. Mac teases me mercilessly about the contents of my pack. I load it up with whatever I find lying around the house being more concerned with weight than subject matter. Mac asks, "Have you seen the refried beans? I know I bought a can of tomatoes," and "Where's the rubbing alcohol?" My first pack weighed about twenty pounds and I have worked up to thirty-five. I don't do a "practice pack" when Aja is around because it embarrasses her. "My friends will see you and think that you are homeless," she pleads.

Today I venture out to Garland Ranch Park in Carmel Valley for more practice and my first solo day hike. I feel anxious about walking alone but really need to get into shape. The pack feels good as I leave the car and step onto the trail. It's a gorgeous Carmel Valley summer day. As I leave the river and the meadow, the hills begin and the trees shade the sun. I am alone out here. My eyes scan the woods, glancing over my shoulders, wondering who I might meet, or what if a mountain lion appears or what to do if I get hurt? I'm afraid. I want to get rid of this fear yet remain aware and careful. I hike uphill for about two hours, mostly on well-marked trails, then the view opens up to a panoramic of Carmel Valley stretching out to the sea.

When I reach the top of the world, I discover still one more hill that leads up to a vacated fire outlook tower. The trail thins and disappears in places. Determined to get to that tower I climb rocks and thrash through the bushes. The trail diminishes with one last stretch. Between the tower and me lie about twenty yards straight uphill and a barbed wire fence with a sign that warns, *NO TRESPASSING*. I try to wriggle through the fence but both the pack and I won't fit. The pack won't mind if I leave it here, so I take it off and prop it up next to the fence. "Stay," I command, then wriggle through the barbed wire. When I reach the top of the world, the view is magnificent and well worth the hike. As I round to the other side of the abandoned tower, a dead-end road appears; a lovely, wide, driveable red dirt road that lets me know mankind has been here before. I don't see any cars but so much for the pioneer spirit.

The solo hike feels delightful. My pack and I make it home safely and my self-esteem notches up.

July 1, Saturday ○ ♌
A Walk

Within our dreams and aspirations we find our opportunities.
— Sue Ebaugh

Mac and I set off for a *walk* in Toro Park near Salinas. It is time for a "practice pack." I pocket a small pencil and some paper to write down those thoughts that come in when I hit that stride and sweat that sweat. As I load up my pack and start off on the trail, I suddenly recall a thought that I had a long, long time ago when I was a child. I remember wanting to walk from Mexico to Canada. *Where does a Little One get a thought like that?* Forgetfulness is not so bad because it allows one to think thoughts again that have gotten lost. Through four or five miles of cow pies and whipping wind I fantasize and plan walking from Mexico to Canada.

July 2, Sunday ○ Virgo ♍
PCT

Man is what he believes.
— Anton Chekhov

This memory of my childhood desire to hike from Mexico to Canada fuels hours of entertainment. Mac suggests a couple of books to read: *Journey on the Crest* by Cindy Ross and *The Thousand-Mile Summer* by Colin Fletcher. I go to the library and find both of them. *Journey on the Crest*, about the Pacific Crest Trail, was written and walked by a woman, so I start reading it first. A few chapters in I comment to Mac, "This woman complains about everything. The highlight of her walking seems to be when she leaves the trail and goes into the little towns to re-supply, eat hamburgers, and drink milkshakes. This was her joy. Sometimes she hooked up and walked with other hikers. Then she blamed her discomforts and displeasure on everyone else but herself." I keep reading expecting her to become enlightened. I wait for her to realize and bathe in awe of the beauty surrounding her. I wait. I read. I keep reading. She continues to complain. She even quits hiking at one point, returns home, gets married, and resumes her hike two years later with her new husband.

July 8, Saturday ☽ Scorpio ♏
Walking In

One is not born a woman, one becomes one.
> — Simone de Beauvoir

I finish reading *Journey on the Crest* while Mac and I drive on the long and bumpy dirt road that leads to the trailhead in Dinkey Lakes Wilderness. With Cindy Ross hovering in my head, I hope to have a better time than she did.

We reach the trailhead and finish packing our packs. The day is warm and beautiful with a clear blue sky. We secure the car and hit the trail. My mind begins to wander. Days ago, I watched a documentary about Native Americans. Something I heard rings loud over all of Cindy Ross' bitching, "The Native Americans don't believe in selling land. They say that the land does not belong to us; rather we belong to the land." The last part, *we belong to the land,* fills my heart as I step into a new chapter of being.

The trail follows a creek and climbs up. Flowers, ponds, waterfalls, . . . it is gorgeous out here! I stop to touch the velvet petals on a beautiful bright orange lily. I love it out here. Where is my camera? Wildflowers everywhere! This is heaven. And oh, the fragrance, the flowers, the pines, . . . all fills the air. God is the artist here and the gardener. Dinkey Lakes Wilderness is home to landscapes that man could only dream of re-creating, perfect in every way. *I want to hike the wilderness, take pictures and write a book called, "The Sierra Garden Tour."* This fantasy occupies my mind for miles and lightens my load. I see it. I want to do this. I want to spend seasons out here. I LOVE it.

We walk along for miles, passing creeks, lakes, over the hills and through the woods. I feel at home out here. The wind, the woods, all make sense to me. Home. I am home. This is peaceful. We hike in and up about five miles to a little lake called Thousand Island Lake nestled in the lap of three huge peaks, The Three Sisters. Their reflection in the lake could be a painting, if I were a painter. We drop our packs to look for a campsite. The water is ice cold. The lake is at about 9,000 feet and full of fish.

We set up our tent. My head hurts and I feel weird. We spread out our sleeping bags inside the tent to fluff 'em up a bit. My body gets dizzy when I stand back up. "I don't feel good," and describe the symptoms.

"Uh-oh. You might have altitude sickness. If you don't feel better we'll have to go back down to a lower elevation. Altitude sickness can be fatal." He offers some aspirin. I take it, drink some water and lay down in the tent. This is awful. It feels like a combination MSG headache, morning sickness, and a hangover. I don't want to leave but I feel terrible. Today we went from sea level to 9,000 feet in about seven hours. Maybe too much too quickly? I try to meditate.

Thoughts roll in. My whole life I've always felt out of place. My family was dysfunctional, big time. To remedy childhood woes, I sought counseling after my divorce. My life had been a living hell. In school I never felt like I fit in. I never excelled as an employee. I'm good, honest and hard working but always felt on the *outside* of things. Now, . . . being out here in the wilderness, backpacking in God's world, . . . now I understand. All of my life has been lived in a human-made world of human-made buildings, schools, roads, houses, laws, politics, streets, television, etc., . . . always surrounded by the works of man. Out here I understand, . . . the wind, the flowers, the water, the sky, the trees, the critters . . . . I am home.

After an hour resting in the tent, my well-being returns.

We hike up to a rock ledge to watch the sunset. Earlier today, a fire many miles away by Huntington Lake left a smoky residue on the distant horizon that paints a colorful evening display. To view the sunset we sit on a rock ledge next to a beautiful, stunted pine tree that grows in a hole in the rock. How can it exist? It grows in rock, not the forest floor of dirt. It is such a tiny thing, surely inhibited by living in and on a rock, being the quintessential bonsai pine. We sit and let the sunset entertain us with a spectacular evening show of light and color.

As light fades, an idea comes to mind. Not regularly a morning person, I enthusiastically vow, "I will rise in the morning before the sun, come here again to this same special spot and sit next to this little pine tree to witness the waking of the wilds. Wanna join me?"

Mac rolls his eyes and says, "We'll see."

We'll see usually means *probably not.*

As the light fades into darkness we wander back to camp. Tired from a day of walking we go right to sleep.

A bright light wakes me. Is it sunrise? Am I late? I peek out the tent door. Ah-h, it's the moon. The moon is in its last phase and it is probably about 2 a.m. The heavenly light brightens the night. I return to sleep.

July 9, Sunday ○ Sagittarius ♐
The Little Tree

Life shrinks or expands in proportion to one's courage.
— Anaïs Nin

I wake again while it is still dark, grab my flashlight, a sitting pillow, and scramble up the rocks to the magic ledge. I find the little bonsai tree and sit. As I wait for the light a profound silence embraces my awareness. I have never heard anything (or nothing) so quiet. We sit in the silence for a very long time. Then a sound, like Morse code, starts up. How could I be hearing Morse code? Is it my imagination? More silence. More time. A morning birdsong breaks the spell. A bird flaps by. A jet. I hear a jet but where is it? I look toward the sound that gets louder and louder and heads straight toward my head. A bumblebee? Yes. No jet.

Light begins to replace the dark. Behind me sits The Three Sisters. Which peak will catch the first pink glow of the morning light? Across the valley stand rocky mountains waiting for their daily dose of warm.

As the light unfolds we soak it all in. It seems like it takes a long time for the light to appear above the jagged peaks on the horizon. We sit and wait. Where is that morning star? Ah-h, what an incredible view! Oh, the beauty. Far away across a plateau, rocky peaks glow pink. One-by-one the light bathes the peaks and dribbles down the mountainsides.

"There you are! GOOD MORNING SUN! Thank you." We sit and share the warmth of the morning star.

I turn to The Little Tree and say, "You are so lucky. You get to see this every day."

Then, The Little Tree says back to me, "You're pretty lucky; you have a choice."

My jaw drops. The Little Tree talked! I gasp a deep breath, heave a heavy sigh, then bow my head. "Oh Little Tree. Thank you for your wisdom and grace."

I sit and stay as long as I can.

Then I turn to say goodbye, "Thank you, Little Tree. I have to go now. I will come back to visit you again some day."

After breakfast we hike up one of The Three Sisters to its summit, elevation over 10,000 feet. Oh, the beauty. I love backpacking. Everything I need is on my back. This is awesome! I can go anywhere.

July 10, Monday ☽ ♐
Home?

Change is the constant, the signal for rebirth, the egg of the phoenix.
— Christina Baldwin

Re-entry to the human-made world proves challenging. Now I understand why Mac always eats dinner on the porch when he returns from backpacking trips. I feel best outside under the open the sky. We take dinner outside to eat on the porch but where are the birdsongs? All I hear are cars, trucks, sirens, jets and planes. It's even too loud to hear the wind blowing through the trees. I miss being *out there* in the wildness. I'm feeling homesick and wish to go back out again.

Mac finds an article in *CitySports* magazine about a woman named Sandra Johnson who hiked 2667 miles on the Pacific Crest Trail (PCT) from Mexico to Canada solo in a little more than six months. She married when she was nineteen years old, had three kids, a thirty-year marriage and didn't start hiking till she was 49 years old. She's now 59. She writes, "It's much safer for a woman to walk alone through the forest than downtown Los Angeles."

Animals, rugged terrain and weather aren't nearly as scary to me as some people. I'd much rather deal with the elements of nature than the variables of mankind. City life isn't for me; give me the great outdoors. *Thank you, Sandra Johnson, for hiking the PCT and sharing your story. You are an inspiration.*

Getting back to work after being out there proves difficult. Today I drove around town dressed in my suit with panty hose and high heels, stressed out to the max. I saw myself as being the woman I never wanted to become. I don't know if I'm willing to do this anymore. I want my hiking boots.

PART III — *Take A Hike*

July 18, Tuesday ◯ ♈
My Hero

And once I had escaped the works of man there was no more inhumanity.

— Colin Fletcher, *The Thousand-Mile Summer*

Returning from my first backpacking trip I launched into reading *The Thousand-Mile Summer*. After reading Cindy Ross' rendition of her walk on the Pacific Crest Trail, Mr. Fletcher's poetic account was refreshing and inspiring. Fletcher chose an alternate route of the PCT and hiked solo. The above quote appears early in the book as he leaves civilization and enters the desert wilderness of southern California. I latch onto this quote relieved that someone else feels like I do.

I savored Fletcher's masterpiece as I would enjoy a finely prepared meal, relishing the exquisite combinations and variety. He authored the hiker's bible, *The Complete*

Walker, another masterpiece. I found Fletcher's *Learn of the Green World* audio recording (read by the author) at the local library. Of course I checked it out then listened, re-listened and nearly wore it out before it was due back.

A backpacker friend, Ken, mentioned that Mr. Fletcher lives somewhere in the Monterey Peninsula area. My friend Genie told me that her father used to play tennis with Mr. Fletcher.

Today Mac and I go for a sunset hike down the Big Sur Coast, Highway 1, at Soberanes Creek in Garrapata State Park, about seven miles south of Carmel. It's a lovely, magically varied loop, offering everything from enchanted redwood and California bay laurel groves to soaring hawks, windswept cliffs, delicate wildflowers and panoramic views of the Pacific Ocean. My pencil and paper stay ready to jot down all of those great ideas that usually come in during a walk; ready for ideas that might disappear if I don't write them down as soon as they enter. I've discovered that if I wait to get back to the car or home, the thoughts tend to get lost in the confusion of the human-made world. Sometimes I go for walks simply to clear my mind and to see what comes in.

Soberanes is Colin Fletcher's home turf. On this day, on this walk, a thought comes in. *What if one day I am out walking and here before me on the trail walks Colin Fletcher?* What would I say? Would I say anything? Rumor has it that he's a very private person and hikes to be alone with his thoughts. Would I run up and offer my hand? Would I wink and smile to say that I know who he is and respect his solitude? Would I stumble over my words or stumble over some rocks?

If I were to meet Colin Fletcher . . . , are the only words that I write on my paper today. Nothing else comes in. How odd. Usually, my little paper is covered with scribbles, thoughts, notes, things to do and words to remember whole scenes of my fantasies. But today that's all that I receive. Maybe I should write a poem and call it, *If I Were to Meet Colin Fletcher* . . . .

We return home, shower and dress for a concert at the Sunset Auditorium in Carmel, *The Kronos Quartet.*

It's an excellent performance. At intermission we go outside for air. We walk past two gray-haired men talking and one man's voice strikes a chord in my being. "Mac! Is that Colin Fletcher? Do you know what he looks like? Look! Look!"

"Yes, I think it is."

The familiar Welsh accent from the library audiobook catches my attention.

Go talk with him, . . . the internal conversation begins and I share with Mac. "But I can't," I say in the next breath.

Mac urges me on, "If not now, when?"

I finally walk over and say, "Excuse me, are you Colin Fletcher?"

The man smiles and returns, "Guilty." He corrects my pronunciation of *Colin,* letting me know that I made it sound like a part of the human anatomy.

My resulting embarrassment inspires me to start babbling a-mile-a-minute. I recite the quote from *The Thousand-Mile Summer,* "And once I had escaped the works of man there was no more inhumanity," to the best of my memory. I mention my friend Genie's dad (Colin's former tennis buddy). I don't remember if I tell him about the hike today or the solo notation that I wrote about him, but I hand him my card and say, "I love to play tennis. Call me." I feel so thrilled to meet him.

And what are the chances? . . . *If I were to meet Colin Fletcher* . . . . Ask and ye shall receive.

I haven't written the poem, . . . yet.

July 19, Wednesday ◯ ♉
The California State Lottery

These three instructions, plus meditation, contain the only rule of life that any disciple needs: detachment; realization of God as the Giver; and unruffled patience. As long as we fail in any one of these three, we still have a serious spiritual defect to overcome.

— Sri Gyanamata

Six years ago I had a dream that I became an instant millionaire by winning the lottery. In the dream I bought the ticket at Valnizza's Market, the little neighborhood store catty corner from my house. So I bought my first lottery ticket, *Quick Pick* numbers randomly chosen. I focused on my six numbers. I wrote them out, concentrated and contemplated. I prayed and knew that I was going to win.

I didn't.

The California State Lottery is held every Saturday and Wednesday night at 8 p.m., so I bought another ticket for the next drawing. And since I had put so much energy and faith into the initial *Quick Pick* numbers, I decided to stay with those six numbers.

Time passed and every week, twice a week, I made sure that I bought my numbers.

A year later we moved from that neighborhood. I bought my ticket elsewhere. When I didn't win I thought it might be because I wasn't buying it from Valnizza's. So whenever possible I would venture back to the old stomping grounds to purchase my dream.

In the next couple of years, I began learning to meditate. My understanding of the Universe changed and I changed with it. I found a power higher than myself, God, the cosmic intelligence. Daily meditation began to take priority over other Earthly matters and I found peace. But I still didn't win the lottery. Sometimes I would forget to buy my numbers and once I frantically left the dinner table to pursue the dream. I became obsessed and addicted. I planned and begged and prayed and made deals with the Higher Power, but still I didn't win.

I learned to let go of it. I learned detachment. I learned the value of the one dollar that it took to buy the ticket. I learned greed. I'm still learning patience. Maybe the Universe put the dream in my head to help me learn all the lessons that I've learned since I had the dream.

I've changed so much since I started buying lottery tickets. Meditation prompted me to drop habits like caffeine, alcohol, white sugar, and flesh eating. Basically I'm the same spirit essence I was when I was a little child but with more history.

Tonight's lottery is over $50,000,000. Oh what a prize and oh what this does to my imagination. Since this lottery adventure began, the list of what I would do with the money has changed week-to-week and month-to-month. Last Monday a brand new idea came to mind that was very clear and powerful.

One reason I began meditating arose from reading the book *Autobiography of a Yogi* by Paramahansa Yogananda. He became my spiritual teacher. He founded the Self-Realization Fellowship (SRF) with the Mother Center located in Los Angeles. There's a beautiful building by Lake El Estero in Monterey called Marsh's, an Oriental antique and gift shop surrounded by high walls and bamboo. I'm sensing that it might be a good spot for a SRF annex in Monterey. There's a SRF temple in Los Gatos and one in Berkeley but nothing between Los Gatos and Los Angeles. SRF students here on the Peninsula use as their meeting place a tiny, dark room in Carmel. Yogananda deserves something larger, brighter, bolder and more amiable. So if I win the lottery, I will offer to buy Marsh's and donate it to SRF. Yogananda has helped with the progress of my spiritual evolution and I'd like to give back a gift of appreciation that could facilitate others to self-realization.

I've even enlisted visualization techniques to manifest the event. I bought ping pong balls (like the ones used for the televised lottery drawing) and wrote my numbers on the balls. I've also taped the numbers up on my bathroom mirror so I can give those numbers full attention many times during a day. This method worked successfully in other manifestations, so why not this one?

I believe that I'm going to win the California State Lottery. Maybe not tonight but I will win. Miracles happen.

Through this process I am still learning meditation, detachment, God as the Giver, and patience.

> *patient* [< L. *pati*, endure]
> *en-dure* [< L. *in*,+ *durus*, hard]

Must we humans endure hard times and suffer to receive the gifts of God? I hope not. I don't think that's how life is supposed to be. I won't believe that we're here on Planet Earth to suffer. Aren't we here to evolve human consciousness?

> *hard* [OE. *heard*] 1. firm and unyielding to the touch; solid and compact. 2. powerful [a hard blow] 3. difficult to do, understand, or deal with. (all from *Webster's New World Dictionary*)

> hard [ME; OE *heard*; c. D *hard*, G *hart*, Icel *harthr*, Goth *hardus*; akin to Gk *kratys* strong] (from *The Random House College Dictionary*)

Well, that makes sense. To have patience means to be *strong, solid*. I am learning to be strong and becoming patient. Faith. Trust. Those are strong.

I've been telling everyone to go buy a lottery ticket today. *You can't win unless you play. Somebody is going to win.* I told Mary, the co-owner of Valnizza's Market, that if I win I will give her 5%. She deserves to win. We all do.

July 20, Thursday ☽ ♉
Role Model

When one loves the Giver of gifts more than the gifts, freedom is nigh.
——Paramahansa Yogananda

Today I send my copy of the book *The Secret Life of Plants* (by Peter Tompkins and Christopher Bird) to Jenn, the river guide on our Rogue River trip. On the trip she brought along *The Audubon Field Guide to North American Wildflowers*. We stalked a wild Showy Milkweed together and a couple of other lovely discoveries. I felt she experiences the same joy with plants that I feel. I had read only the first chapter of *The Secret Life of Plants* and found the book thought provoking.

After my walk to the post office I cruise a used bookstore seeking to replace the book for my own. When I leave I follow a man and a little girl to the door. The little girl drops her water bottle and it spins a few feet across the floor. I pause patiently and wait for her to recover. She looks up at me, dips her head shyly and dives for the shins of, who I assume to be, her father. She recovers well and I let them exit first. I pause to look at the books in the window display. The man and the little girl move down the sidewalk at a slow pace. I head for home, going the same direction. They look back at me. Because they are walking slowly, I easily catch up. Out of the blue the man says to me, "That quote in Morgan's [Coffee *&* Tea Shop] is sticking in my head."

"What quote?" I ask, sensing that I am meant to hear what he has to say.

"*Man is what dog thinks God is*," he says and goes silent. Then he says something about having a dog and something about 14 years. "He died a couple of weeks ago."

I feel his energy soften. "I'm sorry."

In an apologetic manner he adds, "Now the quote is probably going to stick in *your* head all day."

"Yep. All day."

So yes, here I am walking and thinking about it. Children think that their parents are God too. One of the scariest moments in my life was when I realized that my young child would believe any answers that I gave to her questions. As a parent I always tried my best to be loving and honest. My child's mind was being programmed with whatever program I chose for her and whatever she chose to trust. From my own childhood I knew that adults do not automatically become sane, loving adults once they beget offspring and that Little Ones are at the mercy of their parents who do not always behave god-like.

As humans on Earth, we have a duty, a responsibility. We belong to the Planet Earth and we have forgotten this. The Europeans came to America and nearly wiped out an entire race of God's precious children, the Native Americans. White man could have learned so much from these people. Instead we, (and I say *we* because I live in the culture that evolved from those days) bulldozed the real people and their lands. We stripped them of their dignity, spirituality and their lives.

I wish I could live like the Native Americans did. They lived in God's country. People in our current culture pay big bucks to vacation in the wilderness and experience the land as the Native Americans lived. Rafting through the Rogue River Canyon I felt them. I felt the peace, joy and community spirit at Solitude Bar. I felt the pain and anger at Battle Bar. I felt the blood. I felt sorry. I also felt the land. I felt the soul of the woods and the osprey, the Great Blue

Herons, the otters, the deer and the bears. Just because we humans have been given more technologically advanced gifts and tools than other inhabitants of Planet Earth, it doesn't mean we have the right to abuse nature. We dam the rivers, slaughter the buffalo, kill the Grizzly and have nearly annihilated the native peoples of this land. What gives us that right? What gives anybody that right?

Man of today lives in fear. We have used our skills and talents to protect ourselves from Mother Nature. I feel that we chose to live on Planet Earth so we could celebrate life and evolve human consciousness. But generally we try our hardest to shield ourselves from everything that is natural to Earth. City life has created a microcosm of human existence that doesn't have to interact with the elements of Earth. Yes, we require protection from life-threatening elements such as tornadoes, earthquakes, hurricanes, fires, floods, heat, cold, viruses, etc. But we keep trying to control, predict and outsmart Mother Nature when we might be able to find peace of mind by becoming more intimate and learning to trust her.

This society drives to the gym, walks, bikes, runs or rows on machines and gets back in their cars to drive home. You can jog on a machine and use technology and the senses to visually replicate any environment, a city, the woods or the shoreline. It seems totally unnatural and a perverse use of our "higher intelligence" to create Virtual Reality Gyms. Why not actually run on the beach or walk in the woods?

As being the highest on the Earth's food chain, we have a responsibility to all other critters on Earth, plant and animal, to protect them. Maybe God put us here to care for the dolphins, the whales, the tarantulas, and the rain forests. We should be here as caretakers, not as abusers of Earth's resources. Maybe the resources were given to us to be used only when necessary. Maybe we were to be used when necessary too. I don't have much expertise in history, philosophy, anthropology, environmental studies or religion but I can feel the injustice in my heart.

I know some humans that I would not want for a master. I hope that if I get reincarnated as a dog, I can choose my master.

> *Our deepest fear is not that we are inadequate. Our deepest fear is that we are powerful beyond measure. It is our light, not our darkness that most frightens us. We ask ourselves, who am I to be brilliant, gorgeous, talented and fabulous.*
>
> *Actually, who are you not to be? You are a child of God. Your playing small doesn't serve the world. There is nothing enlightened about shrinking so that other people won't feel insecure around you.*
>
> *We were born to make manifest the glory of God that is within us. It is not just in some of us, it's in everyone, and as we let our own light shine, we consciously give other people permission to do the same. As we are liberated from our own fear, our presence automatically liberates others.*
>
> — Marianne Williamson, *A Return To Love*

Some people think that the only way they can get power is from other people. This is not true. The inner power and love light comes from the spirit-that-moves-in-all-things. This is a gift that we have the responsibility to use wisely.

Tell your dog that (s)he is a god. Tell your children that they are gods. Tell your employees, patients, clients, students, neighbors, lovers, teachers, parents, politicians, and enemies that they are gods. Tell yourself that you are a god and be not afraid of the light and grace. Find it, follow it, embrace it, . . . often. Give God the love that (s)he gives you, everyday, unconditionally. Give yourSelf the love that God gives you. Act like God. God forgives you. God always has time to listen to you. God is the Giver of gifts. Give God thanks.

So, yes, I will think about that quote today, "Man is what dog thinks God is." In fact it has put me on my high horse and ruffled my feelings. Please let me always conduct myself with dignity and grace in the presence of dogs and all other of God's creatures, from amoebas to humans to zebras.

I find a copy of *The Secret Life of Plants* in another used bookstore down the street. The marked price is $9.95 crossed out, then $2.95 written under it in pencil. That's rather high considering it is a small paperback and the original cover price was only $1.95 (that has been whited out). I figure it is worth $2.95 since the last one cost only 50 cents and I gave it away as a gift. I reach in my pocket to dish out $3.00 and tax as the proprietor says, "That's a dollar and three cents."

"Oh, what a deal. Thank you. Have you read it?" I like to share good books.

"No, not yet. I can't keep it on the shelf long enough."

I feel tickled to get it.

When Mac comes home after work, he walks in with an armload of books. "I have a surprise for you!" he twinkles.

Yes, he too found a copy of *The Secret Life of Plants* in a different used bookstore. I don't remember mentioning to him that I'd been in pursuit of a replacement copy. He's amazing. It is rather coincidental that we should do it on the same day, one month after giving it away. I love coincidences. It's the Universe trying to get our attention. Given enough coincidences we might begin to wonder if indeed some higher power is taking care of the details.

July 22, Saturday ◯ ♊
A New Trail Guidebook

When you and your companion are newly in love, the two of you walk with minds interwoven, and the body enriches everything you see. And that is the best walking of all.

— Colin Fletcher, *The Complete Walker III*

Mac asks, "What would you like to do today?"

"Go for a hike at Mount Madonna," comes out of my mouth.

First we stop by the Sierra Club bookstore on Ocean Avenue in Carmel. We spend at least an hour. Three books leave with me: *The 2 oz. Backpacker* by Robert S. Wood, *Simple Foods for the Pack* by Claudia Axcell, Diana Cooke and Vikki Kinmont, and *Popular Outings of the Monterey Bay Area and Beyond* by the Ventana Chapter of the Sierra Club.

We choose a hike from the last book and drive to Mount Madonna, east of Watsonville on Highway 152. Our hike begins at Sprig Lake and climbs straight uphill for about an hour toward the Mount Madonna County Park campground. This walk is just what I need. I get very restless and obsessive when I need a walk. I've got to go. I must walk. I must get *out there* back into the wilds.

Walking is spiritual nutrition. The body needs food, sleep and exercise. The mind needs input and contemplation. My spirit needs nature and meditation. Mount Madonna provides the perfect backdrop for my whole being.

We hike about five miles in the cool redwood canyons and hillsides, seeing enough to know that we want to come back and explore more again someday.

July 23, Sunday ☼ ♌ / ☽ ♊
A New Way to Walk

Illegal aliens have always been a problem in the United States. Ask any Indian.

— Robert Orben

Today starts out like yesterday, "What would you like to do today?" Mac asks.

"I don't know, what do you want to do?" eager to hear his ideas.

Being Sunday, Mac reads the two Sunday papers we get: the local Monterey County *Herald* and the San Francisco *Chronicle*. I read my new books. We eat bagels and sit in the morning sun discussing our possibilities for the day.

We make our decision at 1:09 p.m. A hike. We gather the necessities. For Mac the necessities appear to be his fanny pack and two water bottles. I pack up *The Audubon Society Field Guide to North American Wildflowers,* water, sunscreens SPF #s 4, 8, 15, and 30 (you never know what might happen), GORP, a lightweight parka, insect repellent, the trail book, my hairbrush, candles, lighter, flashlight, (I couldn't find my snakebite kit), lip balm, and my new backpacker Swiss Army knife. It makes for a ridiculously weighty daypack but I like the weight. It helps to keep me in shape for spontaneous backpacking trips.

We drive down the Big Sur coast on Highway 1 and take the Old Coast Road at Bixby Creek Bridge. We continue beyond where the Little Sur River and the south fork of the Little Sur join at the trailhead. Ah, yes, another day in paradise. The redwood fairy forests are alive with food for my imagination. Wood sorrel, yellow violets, wild thimbleberries and some kind of blue berry, that I sense is not edible, scatter their color about. "If this trail is this lush in July, can you imagine it in the spring time?" The water in the Little Sur sparkles crisp and clear.

After a couple of miles climbing, the trail narrows then dips back down to the creek. We cross. [I must say something about two words: *Creek* and *river.* We call this *Little Sur River.* On the map it's called a *river.* However, anyone from east of the Mississippi River would look at me strangely and laugh if they would hear me call this body of water a *river*. Spending my childhood here we called it a *river*. Then I began to travel. This is really a *creek*.]

Up the creek we come upon a seemingly abandoned camp that looks extremely out of place. There's a bulldozed road widened with a vulgar disregard for tree, rock, or violet. We poke around and discover a black plastic curtain with a toilet behind it. Then another. We come across a whole area that appears to have been ruthlessly cleared then crudely developed. Old refrigerators, stoves, hot water heaters, sinks, all outside and very out of place. "Care not to disturb the wilderness" lies abandoned for an apparent business venture or some extremely deprived, depraved or savage boy scouts. We check everything out, then find the meek resemblance of the continuing trail on the other side of a graveled clearing.

We follow the trail as far as we dare, interrupted and diverted by a high number of fallen trees. We climb and jump, playing like a couple of kids.

Suddenly I hear, "Did you see me sitting here?" a voice from the woods.

I quickly turn. A man sits in a tree, all dressed up in camouflage clothing. He likes being sneaky. "No," I answer.

"Saw a whole pack of wild boar up there a bit," he adds.

Now he's probably trying to scare me out of *his* woods. I take it as truth. *Well, it is time to turn back anyway, isn't it?*

Mac appears and we talk with the man. He and his son backpacked in and they're camping here. We take our leave. Mac walks back on the rocks and crisscrosses the creek. I climb up and walk on the trail. We each find a dandy walking stick amongst the recently strewn timber.

Mac rejoins me on the trail and we settle into a pace. I remember something I read in my new book, *The 2 oz. Backpacker* (a backpacker's field guide cleverly titled because of its weight). The section I remember has to do with a way of walking that the author called the "Indian Step." I pull the book out of my daypack, find the passage, stop Mac and read the description out loud to both of us:

> *Modern Americans tend to walk without swinging their hips. The Indian travels more efficiently. At the end of each step he swings the hip forward as well as the leg, pivoting at the waist. And he leans forward slightly as he walks. The forward lean and turning of the hips lengthens the stride, positions the feet almost directly in front of one another, and minimizes the wasteful up and down movement. The result is a more fluid, floating walk, with less wasted motion. And on easy ground the longer stride produces more speed. The chief disadvantages of the Indian Step are that it is difficult to master, requiring agility and balance; and the advantages are greatest for the unburdened walker.*

Mac tries it but quickly reverts back to his familiar stride and pace. For me it is a true revelation and an efficient addition to my walking skills. The "Indian Step" extends my stride and with that, I'm able to effortlessly keep up with Mac. He stands about six feet two inches and I am five foot three. I used to catch up with him by running on the downhills. Now I have a new tool. *Thanks Mr. Wood.*

As we drive out of the canyon I say, "The Native Americans were the luckiest of people in this world."

"Excuse me?" Mac asks, quite used to my off-the-wall comments but still curious.

"I mean, . . . as long as it lasted. They had this whole, beautiful country, free to travel wherever and whenever they wished. They could live here in Big Sur or in the Sierra or in the Rogue River Valley or the Rockies. They were free to roam anywhere."

Mac adds, "They had no concept of private property. That's how they got into so much trouble. They were used to going where they wanted to go and hunting wherever the game took them."

"I'm so sorry. How can we ever make this right?" I ask.

The more time I spend with nature, the more I feel the Native Americans. They lived as part of the land, part of Mother Nature. The land provided them with everything they needed. I'd like to think they were happy. The Europeans coming to America behaved more savage than the Native Americans.

So whether they had anything to do with the "Indian Step" or not, I'd like to give thanks. The quality of my walking has improved and I look forward to more practice. I wonder what else we could learn from the Native Americans?

July 28, Friday ○ ♌
Soberanes

You must do the thing you think you cannot do.
— Eleanor Roosevelt

Sometimes the hardest part about doing things is getting started. A cut-out *Far Side* cartoon that I've saved since the '80s, is taped on my office wall: A person in pajamas is sitting on the bedside with the rising sun showing through the bedroom window. On the wall directly in front of the person is taped a huge, handwritten sign that says,

"First pants,

THEN

your shoes."

I've known days like that, when small tasks such as eating, sleeping and brushing teeth, must be written down on a list to be acted upon. We've all been down occasionally. Some persons go further down for a longer time. Some persons never get back up.

After work, Mac asks if I want to go for a "walk." The sun is shining bright with clear blue sky. [Summer weather on the Monterey Peninsula is different from regular summer weather of the rest of the world. Since this is my hometown, I never knew what *real* summer weather was until I was twenty-one years old and moved away to Brown County, Indiana, for seven years. Summer weather in Monterey consists of fog or patchy fog. I have seen entire Julys or Augusts completely devoid of blue sky and sunshine. Last month an incredible amount of people died from the heat wave in the rest of this country. Chicago alone lost at least 700 people to heat-related deaths. Hot weather is rare on the Monterey Peninsula. I consider hot weather to be 75° or above. About four days in a year, the temperature might exceed 80°, and this occasionally happens in January or February.]

Mac and I load our walking gear into the car and drive south. We head for Soberanes. We round the bend and my spirit sinks when I see the fog bank sitting on Carmel Hill waiting to jump on us. The fog follows us down Highway 1.

The Soberanes Trail can be an in-and-out that follows the Soberanes Creek up the redwood canyon, or an up-and-down the Rocky Ridge Trail, or a 4.5-mile loop that begins, or ends, on the Rocky Ridge Trail. We choose to begin there. The trail goes up, up, up. I see a few ticks, a lot of lizards, a surprisingly abundant amount of wildflowers for the end of July, a covey of quail and a lot of stink bugs.

At one point I tell Mac, "You know, the good thing about hiking in the fog is that we can't see how far up we still have to hike." We ascend higher into the fog and soon lose sight of Highway 1. I have never been up here on a foggy day and it is quite different. Without fog, the view of the coastline is breathtaking. We soon appreciate the cool mist, however. We'd really be sweating if it was hot and sunny. Up, up, up.

The higher we climb, the brighter it gets. Then, out-of-the-blue, . . . sky. Blue sky. Soon, we walk out of the fog. The emergence into brightness feels like morning time. Here we are, . . . above the fog. It's like we're in an airplane or jet. Being above the fog is much more fun than being in the fog. A whole different world exists down there unaware of the open blue sky up here on the hilltops.

We hike to an overlook where the fog below creeps into side valleys and canyons, molding itself to the arched shape of Monterey Bay to the north. The humid mass extends to the west across the Pacific as far as we can see. We are at the top of the world. Hawks soar then dive for dinner. I could stay up here a long, long time. Days, months, years. What a great place this would be for a house. What a great place this is for a public hiking trail.

The sun begins dipping toward the fog line. We continue the loop eastward, then south. Down, down, down. Sometimes hiking down is just as hard as hiking up, only different. Mac jumps at a bend of the trail and I stop. Between us, stretching out of the bushes lies the front end of a brown, white and black snake.

"Is it a rattler?" I ask.

Mac carefully pokes and peeks through the surrounding flora and responds slowly, "No. I don't think so. I don't see any rattles."

"Are you sure?"

He looks again, "Yep. I see the end of its tail and I don't see any rattles. He's long, though."

I take a closer look leaning in as close as I dare. "Okay, how do I get by it?"

"I did it."

"Yeah, but you didn't see him until you were passing over him." I decide and choose the overhead route, too, thinking that if I step in front of him (or her), he (or she) might dart toward my foot and startle me. I gather some courage and walk over it.

Mac reports, "It stuck its little tongue out as you made your pass."

I pause to view its entire body and feel glad that I passed first then looked. It is a long one, probably 3½ feet. Whoa!

A little further down the trail we meet a solo hiker traveling the loop in the opposite direction. We warn him about the snake, give him a general location and tell him that it is not a rattlesnake. We dip back into the fog and into the shadowy canyon losing warmth and light. "Goodbye Sun. And thank you for the beautiful day."

At the bottom of the ridge trail begins Soberanes Creek Canyon, an enchanted redwood and California bay laurel grove. As we descend into the forest, I feel at peace and secure. I thank Mac for the walk. "This is just what I needed." Then a thought comes to mind: *Could hiking be good therapy for something like suicide prevention?* Sometimes it can help if a person steps outside of his or her living environment to observe their situation more objectively. Quality time with Mother Nature could help.

This line of thinking occupies my mind for a while. Then a thought comes in: *Write a short story about it, using fiction as a vehicle to spread the idea.*

"But I don't write fiction." I mumble back quietly.

You can try, a little voice responds.

The internal conversation continues for the rest of the walk. It seems to be a conversation between different parts of my being: The ego, the child, the spirit, the parentally programmed voice, the adult, and the culturally programmed voice, . . . to name a few. These conversations can take place with many voices or just a couple of them.

I continue to think about the subject matter after we come home. I talk with my friend Genie about the dilemma. "I don't write fiction. I journal, . . . write the truth, as I know it. I won't lie."

"Fiction isn't lying. I'm going to tell you what you always tell me, *Don't be afraid of that creative part of you. Just go do it.* You know, the hardest part about creativity is just getting started. Don't get attached to the results of your endeavor. I'm sensing that's what you're thinking. You might be so worried about what other people are going to think about your creation, that it stops you from doing it. Writing fiction is storytelling. It's creative and fun."

She's so right. I don't allow myself to develop my ideas using fiction because I'm afraid of the result. Whether I'm afraid that the piece might be garbage or afraid that I might get carried away in my own fantasy world, the reason is still fear.

When I was going through counseling after the divorce, I reached the point where it became a pleasure to discover a new fear, a new denial. Finding and identifying a fear meant that I could experience the joy and liberation of overcoming it. After mastering a few of the blatant and obvious fears, I looked for those deep dark hidden ones. I invited them to show their beastly heads. I fought them and won. I must look at this as yet another fear emerging into my awareness. Fear of creativity.

Thanks, Genie. You are an Angel of Truth.

July 31, Monday ☽ ♍
Environmental Fragility

Humorists always sit at the children's table.
— Woody Allen

I'm in the backyard watering my garden and minding my own business. The rumble of a large moving van driving by dominates the scene. Its enormity triggers an irritating car alarm. The disturbance continues long enough to give everyone in the neighborhood a chance to check if the warning requires a response. Finally, the noise stops.

A mockingbird sings. I love mockingbirds and their sweet songs. Then the bird begins to imitate the sirens, beeps, and horns it just heard from the car alarm. This feels both entertaining and disturbing. The talented songbird's creativity amuses me and touches my heart. But it disturbs me probably because of the persistent restlessness that I feel for returning to a more natural environment. The longer I live in a city, the more ludicrous human behavior appears. Like the mockingbird, I believe that human behavior can be directly influenced by the immediate daily environment. Living in a natural environment, do we become more natural?

After dinner, without even discussing the matter with Mac, he brings to my attention an article from last week's *San Francisco Chronicle* in the "Earth Week" section entitled, *Tone Deaf:*

> *"Songbirds living near British motor ways are losing the ability to produce their true natural mating and territorial songs because the discordant roar of traffic has confused their auditory senses," the British Ecological Society announced. "Birds, ranging from wrens and blue tits to woodcocks and pheasant, are so off-key that they cannot ward off intruders from their territory or attract a mate," according to research published in the society's journal. The report quotes a Dutch study that says that noise pollution also affects the reproduction of birds living within two or three miles of major highways by drowning out the chirps and coos to prospective partners.*

I feel sad to read this and glad that I am not the only one concerned with man's effects on Earth's creatures. What to do about it is a whole *nuther* question. What do we do? What can we do? How strange to be out backpacking in the wilderness, far away from the maddening crowd, and be serenaded by a mockingbird imitating the beeps, sirens, and honks of a car alarm.

August 3, Thursday ☽ ♏
Love – Love

There is a crack in everything. That's how the Light gets in. That's how the Light gets in.

— Leonard Cohen

Colin Fletcher calls. His regular tennis buddy can't play and he asks if I'm available. YES! I am so excited! I get to play tennis with Colin Fletcher! I would also love to go on a hike with him. I'll keep dreaming.

We meet at the Carmel Valley Racquet Club. I haven't played in a while and I'm kind of in an emotional funk, so I'm not at my best. But happiness prevails. I try to keep up with him. It's so much fun and he's a great tennis player! How old is he? He must be in his 70s.

During the cool down time after play, I watch as he transforms from Fletcher the tennis player to Fletcher, the man. He changes his shirt and hat, takes off his glove and knee wrap, and does a number of little things preparing for re-entry to the non-tennis world. As he does all of this, I sit and listen. He tells stories. He's a storyteller. I feel mesmerized by his Welsh accent. The words he chooses are colorful and deliberate. The stories flow and I listen. I sit on the ground listening like a child to a man of great humor, experience and wisdom (though he would probably deny the *wisdom* part and has claimed himself as a *surly Welsh bastard full of hot air*). I feel in the presence of someone very special.

In the course of the post tennis talk, the topic of astrology surfaces. Then he says, "What sign do you think I am? Not that I believe in that sort of nonsense."

I couldn't guess.

"Pisces," he says, "March 14th."

"So am I. March 9th."

"Sometimes I tell people the wrong sign just to hear them say, *I knew it! I knew you were a Sagittarius,* or whatever sign."

Kindred Pisces Spirits. Could this explain the closeness that I feel with him? Does he feel it too? Could we be like astrologically related? Even though I'm out-of-my-seat curious, I resist asking his birth year.

As we talk of our selves and our lives he says, "I tend to take walks to sort things out and solve problems. This in itself is not unusual, many people do that, I'm sure. *The walk,* . . . from Mexico to Oregon, . . ." [that he chronicled in his book, *The Thousand-Mile Summer*], "was instigated, or inspired, by the question of whether or not to ask a certain lady if she would marry me." He pauses.

I sit, wide-eyed waiting in suspense.

"After the walk, we married." He takes more silence.

I wait.

"A later walk, that prompted the book, *The Man Who Walked Through Time*, was initiated after our divorce."

We make a date to play tennis again. Sweet!

I oftentimes go for a walk when things need sorting out but Colin's walks are well planned and quite extensive. This is what I find fascinating: I understand. This man is a gem, a phenomenon of nature. Astrology. I want to know what year he was born, so I can figure out his planetary aspects.

Back home after dinner, I decide to start reading his book, *The Man Who Walked Through Time*, about his solo walk following the Colorado River through the entire length of the Grand Canyon National Park. Within a few pages appears this sentence, ". . . I grasp this date fairly firmly: I was born in 1922." A gift. I've been given another gift. Oh what fun!

PART IV — *Sierra Garden Tour*

August 4, Friday ☽ ♏
Chain Lakes, Day One

In every work of genius we recognize our own rejected thoughts; they have come back to us with a certain alienated majesty.

— Ralph Waldo Emerson

We're on our way to a three-day backpack trip in the Sierra Nevada Mountains, California. Today's destination is Chain Lakes, a wilderness area in the southeastern area of Yosemite National Park. We're driving through Madera, Highway 145 east, Highway 41 past Bass Lake, then to Chiquito campground/trailhead in the Sierra National Forest. I'm so excited.

Mac is leaving for his annual backpack with the boys on August 19th. This weekend trip is a "practice pack" for him and a treat for me. I'd love to go with the boys but they won't let me. *No chicks allowed.* Oh well, maybe someday.

Whoops? I forgot to buy a lottery ticket. Mac stops at a funky liquor/QuikStop corner store in Los Baños to buy my ticket and satisfy my obsession. He gently teases me but never complains about my idiosyncrasies. I appreciate this.

We arrive at Bass Lake close to 2 p.m. in search of a wilderness permit. We need to get on the trail soon. The Bass Lake sub-station employee directs us to backtrack to the Batterson Ranger Station a couple of miles back up the road. We retrace our route and experience a stuck-in-traffic construction delay. I feel responsible for misleading us to Bass Lake. When Mac drives, I'm the navigator and it was my call to go for the ranger sub-station at Bass Lake. Mac is feeling irritated but remains calm. I keep telling myself, *There's a reason for this detour. Everything will be all right.*

We finally find the Batterson Ranger Station, go inside and Mac waits in line. I stand back to observe the two older ladies (older than me) running the office. A woman walks in and asks me if this is where she can get a firewood permit. I have no idea. A ranger walks through the hallway traveling from office to office. "Ask him," I suggest.

The firewood permit lady talks the ranger's ear off about things I'm sure he doesn't wish to hear: Goats, blue ribbons, Los Angeles, antique butter churns. She talks on and on while I mentally send messages to the ranger, *I'm not with this woman. I am here for a wilderness permit.*

With a break in the soliloquy, I ask the ranger, "How's the road to Chiquito trailhead?"

"Quartz Mountain trailhead?" he looks relieved to discuss something he knows about. We walk over to the laminated map on the wall. Quartz Mountain, instead of Chiquito trailhead, is up a different road that would cut our hiking time by miles and hours. "Do you plan on camping at Chain Lakes tonight?" he asks as he looks at his watch.

I nod *yes*.

"Then I'd go up the Sky Ranch Road to Quartz Mountain trailhead," he points on the map as he speaks.

I trust him.

Mac joins us and agrees that the ranger's plan looks good.

"Thank you," I say to the ranger, who appears eager to get to his office.

Only the two older ladies, Mac and I are left in the office. I turn to the ladies, "Can I ask you a question?" I don't wait for a response, "What about the bears? Have you seen any bears?"

The ladies look at each other. One speaks, "We get bears right here. You see that house up there?" Both ladies get out of their chairs and we shift around the office so they can point out the house up on the hill. "Just last week a bear kept circling that house, day after day. One day the guy who lives up there opened his front door and a bear stood looking at him right in his eyes. He went back into the house, got a pot and a wooden spoon and started clanging the pot to scare that bear away."

"Then one time," the other lady starts, "another bear went into these folk's garage and the door shut. When the folks came home they heard some noise and. . . ."

I listen.

"Just be sure to put all of your food up in a tree. Also put up toothpaste, sunscreen, lip balm, perfumes, . . . anything that smells that they might think is food." [NOTE: This was before food vaults were required in Yosemite.]

I knew all that. We thank them for their help and head for the door.

"Oh, and don't forget your insect repellent. Reports say that mosquitoes are abundant up at Chain Lakes."

So, . . . a change of plans. It looks like it was a good thing that we had to backtrack. Sky Ranch Road is right across the highway and off we go.

The roads leading to trailheads, at least the ones I've traveled, start off like regular roads. Then they gradually get more narrow, then they get bumpy, then dirt, then a parking spot and then the trail. Sky Ranch Road goes up, up, up. Snow banks appear alongside the road. Mac has to do some fancy mud maneuvers. Then we drive through fallen trees cut just wide enough for a car to squeeze through.

We finally find the trailhead parking area at about 4:30 p.m., much later than we planned. We pull out our packs to get them ready and finish the last-minute checklist: Change into hiking boots, arrange the car contents to hide stuff from bears, adjust pack straps and load 'em up.

A silver-gray BMW appears and parks. A young man gets out and speaks to us, "Hi. Are you from Monterey?"

"Yes. How did you know that?" I respond.

"I am too. The ladies at the ranger station told me that someone else from Monterey had just been in to get a permit."

"Where you going?" Mac asks.

"Chain Lakes," he smiles.

I get excited, "That's where we're going!"

I detect no excitement from his face.

"Are you hiking solo?" I ask.

"Yep."

I sense that he is looking more for solitude in the wilderness than company. Now I feel bad that we are headed for the same spot. *What a coincidence.*

He gathers his gear quickly and starts toward the unmarked trail. "Sandy. My name is Sandy."

"I'm Mac."

"Ellen."

We all shake hands.

"Have fun!" and off he walks.

We continue packing and each eat an orange.

A few minutes later, Sandy returns. "Well that's not it. The trail goes fine for a while then stops in a wall of forest." He pulls out his map, checks it and fusses with his pack. A few minutes later he takes off again.

I sense that he wants to get to the lakes before us, probably so he can get his choice of campsites. We wish him well and I hope that he doesn't get lost out there.

Mac pulls out the topography map. We think that the trailhead might actually be behind us. Its location could be blocked from vision by the parked car up the drive. Mac goes off to check it out while I finish with my pack.

Mac comes back in a few minutes and says that it looks promising. We load our packs onto our backs and Sandy reappears from the opposite direction.

"I went down there, found a trail, then it stopped. I went back, then up the road and back here."

We tell him our plan. He hasn't been that way yet, so he elects to try and walk with us.

Down the dirt road a lovely trailhead marker greets us. We walk and talk for a while, then I excuse myself and lag behind. I have to go potty. Sandy takes off and Mac says he'll wait for me up ahead.

The trailhead elevation is 8050 feet. Our first jaunt is downhill with Chain Lakes about five miles away.

At about 1.5 miles we come to Chiquito Pass, elevation 8039 feet. The pass borders Sierra National Forest, Ansel Adams Wilderness, and Yosemite National Park. Snow banks and snowmelt marshes greet us. Our trail sign, standing halfway under water, peeks out of the middle of a pond. A log juts out over the pond and I offer to take a picture of Mac next to our trail sign. He adjusts the camera, hands it to me and says, "Okay, just stand on this spot and shoot." He walks around a tree and steps onto the log that reaches out over the water. Suddenly, mosquitoes appear, swarm, surround me and begin to attack my skin. I swat frantically and as soon as Mac strikes a pose I quickly snap the shutter.

We pull out the *Repel 100®,* a maximum-strength insect repellent, 95% *DEET* and I put some on. We hurry up the trail and the mosquitoes follow.

Because of the high altitude and a long winter in the Sierra, it is springtime in August. The wild blue lupines are soft and young. Many plants are still buds. We hurry through the gorgeous Sierra gardens, swatting all the way.

The trail dips down to cross a little creek. The lower we go the mushier the ground gets. The wetter it gets, the more mosquitoes appear. They don't seem to land quite as often if I walk quickly, so I step as fast as I can. Fortunately we're traveling downhill now.

I hear voices up ahead and see young ones across the creek. Girls, with whistles around their necks, and boys, probably all high school age, approach the creek. They look for a spot to cross.

I can't stop. If I stop, hundreds of vampire mosquitoes will land and suck my blood. The kids all stand swatting the killer bugs. Splish, splash, I don't stop and cross straight through the water. I am so willing to trade wet boots to avoid a mosquito attack. I look back. Mac stops to scout a spot for crossing. I pace up then back down the trail, waiting for him but not daring to stop. He finally crosses and follows me. We continue up the trail. I maintain my swift pace for a bit. Swishing the mosquitoes away, we walk up, up, up. I start getting tired. The scenery is beautiful but it's difficult to give attention to anything but the mosquitoes.

A chapter in the book, *The Autobiography of a Yogi,* involves mosquitoes. Yogananda witnesses his guru, Sri Yukteswar, in meditation, *samadhi,* untouched by the swarming mosquitoes in the room. To Yogananda, Sri Yukteswar doesn't appear to be breathing and his skin is cold to the touch. Yogananda fears that his master has died.

The student covers his teacher's nose and mouth. Convinced that his master has died, Yogananda starts for help. Sri Yukteswar speaks:

> *"So! A budding experimentalist! My poor nose!" Master's voice was shaky with laughter. "Why don't you go to bed? Is the whole world going to change for you? Change yourself: be rid of the mosquito consciousness."*

I begin asking Yogananda and God to let me know how to keep the mosquitoes off of me. I try many different ways to ask for help. The phrase comes to mind, "Mosquitoes don't bother me." I don't believe that saying it will help, however, but I try and try. They do bother me.

The sun drops lower into the trees. Beautiful waterfalls appear; we keep walking. A trail sign says *Chain Lakes 0.9 miles*. Up, up, up. A group of brightly-clothed men in blue and teal fleece sit in a camp near the top of a lovely waterfall. We all wave, then I go back to swatting mosquitoes. The men swat too, so I don't have my own private groupies of kamikaze bloodsuckers.

We reach the first Chain Lake and it is gorgeous with snow banks on the north-facing slopes and rock islands floating in the middle of the lake. We see another group of brightly-clothed adults. A woman stands wearing a mosquito-netted hat. She looks really silly but she is probably not getting bit. Some of the others have net hats too. One man sits crouched in his bright blue plastic rain jacket with the drawstring pulled up tight around his nose. I wave, smile and try to pretend the mosquitoes don't bother me. We decide to go onto the next Chain Lake. Silly as they look, I would love to have some mosquito netting right now.

More beautiful waterfalls appear. I see Sandy, laying out his tent and swatting mosquitoes.

"I'm glad to see you," I say. We wave and keep on going. Mac and I split up, looking for the trail and a campsite. Mac goes uphill away from the lake and I follow the shoreline.

"A trail. I found a trail," I delight.

Mac catches up with me. I see a group of campers to the north. This is not an easy place to get to, Chain Lakes, so I'm surprised to see all the people here. We see another tent and go for higher ground to avoid walking through their campsite. We come upon a group of men with sleeping bags strewn from one end of their campsite to the other. This is a great spot: cleared, level, padded, lakeside, fire pit. Perfect.

Mac asks the campers, "Any good spots up ahead?"

"Yeah, up by the end of the lake." They are all swatting.

"Do you have any wine?" another man asks.

"No. How long are you staying here?" I want their campsite.

"Tomorrow. We'll be leaving tomorrow."

"Great. We'll come back and take your spot. Have fun."

It is getting too dark to be picky about where to set up camp so we quickly find a spot and stop. The site sits close to a roaring waterfall. The mosquitoes continue their feeding frenzy on my flesh. I flash on a scene from Alfred Hitchcock's classic thriller, *The Birds*. I can see the headline now: BACKPACKERS TERRORIZED BY SWARMS OF KILLER MOSQUITOES. Quickly, very quickly, Mac sets up the tent and prepares the bear bag. I set up the kitchen and cook dinner. I light a candle. I light some incense. I light a mosquito coil. I reapply insect repellent. Anything to get rid of those little buggers. We eat quickly, clean up and dive inside the tent, safe at last.

In our haste choosing this spot we settled and ignored that it features a sloping tent site. "Careful. I might roll over you in my sleep," Mac's uphill position and his size hold the advantage.

I strive to be nonviolent but it is now down to them or me. What shall I do? What would Gandhi do about vampire mosquito gangs? The tent is full of these little critters. They land on my face and bite. I cannot sleep like this. I give in and one-by-one begin to kill them, feeling a bit bad about it but not knowing what else to do. Finally, sleep comes.

If we had the atom bomb, we would have used it against the British.
— Mohandas Gandhi, *The Last Phase*, Vol. II, p. 326

I wake up shaking. I'm not shivering from cold. What is this? Why am I feeling this way? I spasmodically shake and shake and can't stop. *DEET?* My Body does not like the *DEET.* I've poisoned myself. TOXIC. I drink a quart of water, . . . shake and shake some more.

Eventually I fall back to sleep.

August 5, Saturday ☽ ♐
Chain Lakes, Day Two

Henry (David Thoreau) spent his life — or earned his life — exploring little more than the area surrounding his hometown Concord.
— Edward Abbey, *Down the River*

I wake up early to attend to my needs. If I could stay in my sleeping bag, believe me I would. It's light out but the sun hasn't peeked over Gale Peak yet. I didn't sleep that well. Maybe the toxic *DEET* and bug bites were too much for my body. Maybe it was the uneven tent site. Mac didn't roll over me but he did end up on top of his Therm-a-Rest® using his sleeping bag, unzipped, as a comforter. It was warm enough even with all of the neighboring snow banks.

When I go outside to go potty, the mosquito killer bugs are waiting for me. I run off, find an appropriate spot and try to take care of business as quickly as I can. The winged critters feast on my exposed flesh.

Since I am already up and out, I walk upstream to explore the waterfall in the daylight and look for a better campsite. I find a possible pathway up the rocks to the next lake, then return to the tent to escape the thirsty insects.

I warn Mac, "Don't go out. They're still there, waiting."

When we finally get up, we soon discover that the mosquitoes don't bite as long as we stay in the direct sunlight. I suggest that before breakfast we take a walk upstream to the third lake and maybe find a new campsite.

We take off upstream, up the rock wall, up the rock ledge, up, up, up. We reach the Upper Chain Lake in a short time. Most of the lake is still frozen. It sits white with snow nestled on the lap of Gale Peak. Big trout swim in and out underneath the ice. In the distance we note a peak not visible from the lower elevations. We guess it might be Merced Peak. Compass and map reading skills would come in handy right now.

We scout the area, throw some snowballs and find a couple of dandy spots to set up camp that seem to be free of mosquitoes. But of course, we are in sunlight. We descend back to our campsite to pack for a move.

"I wonder if that men's group has left yet?" Mac twinkles.

"I'll go check." I take off down the trail on a scouting mission. Unsure of their exact location, I walk quietly and slowly, peeking over the next rock and around the next tree. Do I hear voices? I look. A ring-tailed cat skitters around the rocks trying to get the attention of a yellow-bellied marmot who is ignoring it. The marmot walks, with a kind of a rolling waddle, around the fire ring, scavenging for leftovers. I stop, never having seen a ring-tailed cat in the wilds, but it quickly disappears as soon as it senses my presence. The men are gone, too. The campsite is ours if we want it and get it before anyone else does. The site is a prize, a special spot, and it will go fast, since it is Saturday morning. I don't have anything with me to claim the spot for us, so I quickly run back to tell Mac that it is available.

We talk briefly then decide to move. It isn't far but we have to move quickly to stake it as ours. I load up the kitchen.

Put on your boots, says a little inside voice.

Impatient to get to the new site, I ignore the little voice and carry my pack over to the new campsite without putting on my boots, wearing just my flip-flops. Mac stays to break down the tent. I hurry and pray all the way over to let the site still be vacant.

The camp is ours. Even the marmot has gone. A puff of smoke escapes from the fire pit. Home. We find a home. I plop my pack down in the new kitchen site and begin unpacking. A big noise startles me. As I turn, in walks Mac, cigar in his smiling mouth, carrying his backpack and the tent that he has wrapped around the extended ten-foot-long tent poles. We set up camp, eat breakfast, slather ourselves with sunscreen, strip to shorts, sit in the sun and enjoy paradise.

Mac sits and reads the latest *Backpacker* magazine. He laughs and shows me an advertisement for a shirt with a hood and a mosquito-netted face cover. It might look silly but who cares, I'd wear it.

It's a hot afternoon. I'm sitting on my Therm-a-Rest® with the Merced Peak quadrant topographic map, a compass and the book, *Staying Found* by June Fleming. I'm determined to learn how to read a compass. If I'm going to spend any time out here, I'd better learn how to use the tools. I'm tending a "smoke fire." If yesterday had been my first backpacking trip, it probably would have been my last. As long as I sit in the sun or next to the smoky fire, the mosquitoes don't bother me. But I have to watch my backside. Also, they don't seem to bite through the synthetic fleece pants and pullover.

Mac is off somewhere taking pictures. I sit by the lake, reading and writing. It's so beautiful. The lake, peaks, snow, marmots, birds, trees, sky, sunlight, . . . everything is perfect. I don't want this day to end. This is it. I love being out here. I know we have to go home tomorrow. Mosquitoes and all, backpacking is still the best.

Before dinner, we walk down the trail to scope out our exit options. It was tricky coming into this lake area and we're looking for a better route out. We take in some views and try using the compass. Mac is learning too. I *will* learn.

We make our way back to camp, start dinner and feed the fire. I finally accept that this day will end. Mosquitoes are back in full force. Buzz, buzz, and buzz. The fleece keeps some of them from biting but they still land and they still buzz. I don't want to use the *DEET* anymore. It feels toxic. I put some on my clothing but not on my skin.

Dinner conversation revolves around mosquitoes. "If everything has a purpose here on Earth then what is the purpose of a mosquito? What does it do? And who or what do they bite when humans are not around?"

When I lived in Indiana, I became familiar with a certain species of milkweed that always grew near poison ivy. If I got a poison ivy rash I would break off a piece of the milkweed stem, put its milky-white substance on the outbreak and the poison ivy would dry up. All the locals knew about the plant but I don't remember its name. Perhaps there's a plant here in this forest that is a natural mosquito repellent or at least soothes the itch of the bites. Herbal remedies rule!

Sitting around the fire helps a little, but we eat quickly, clean up, and dive into our little tent. What a relief to be safe. About a dozen skeeters make it inside the tent with us. Mac spots them with the flashlight and I smack 'em. I can't believe what a killer I've become. At home I catch bugs and spiders in jars and take them outside to set them free. I've even yelled at ants ordering them out of my house rather than resorting to poisons. My survival side shows its ugly head. I feel bad, but not that bad. They were driving me nuts.

We go to bed early, not yet 9 o'clock. Mac reads an article about field testing backpack ovens. He reads some passages out loud and drools over descriptions and pictures of cinnamon rolls and pesto pizza baked on the trail. I'm reading *The 2 oz. Backpacker* by candlelight. Happy to be here, soon we read ourselves into slumberland.

August 6, Sunday ☽ ♐
Chain Lakes, Day Three

Nurture your mind with great thoughts, for you will never go any higher than you think.

— Benjamin Disraeli

At home Mac usually wakes up first and I sleep. In the wilds, I always wake up first. This morning I wake first and "pitter" around as much as one can inside a two-person tent. I brush my hair, meditate, read, wash my face and read some more. I don't want to go *out there* and face those little biting critters again. I reach for the *Repel 100®* and see in bold letters the warning: **MAY DAMAGE FURNITURE FINISHES, LEATHERS, PLASTICS, PAINTED SURFACES, AND WATCH CRYSTALS.** I will not put this on my skin again.

Mac wakes up and slides into his fleece pullover and pants.

I panic. "You're not going out there, are you?"

He begins slathering his exposed flesh with insect repellent. "I have to."

"I'm not going out till the sun hits the tent."

"OK." He leaves. He sacrifices himself as breakfast to the waiting predators. He's gone for a while then returns with war reports. "Not bad, . . . if you put *DEET* all over." He hops back in the tent, stuffs his sleeping bag and starts packing up.

"You're going back out?"

"Yep."

"Darn." Then I'll have to get up too. I put on my fleece. As I pull on my right boot, significant pain shoots through my arch. I wriggle it around, assessing the damage then lace up the boot as tight as possible. I leave the safety of the tent. He was right; it's not too bad.

We take our time with breakfast, pack up and leave our camp. I don't want to go. I want to stay. The sun is high and warm and, . . . no mosquitoes.

The trail is beautiful. We meet two young men who are out exploring the lake. Their tent is pitched on a tiny peninsula, a perfect spot. We had seen someone fly fishing last evening and ask if it had been one of them.

"Yes, but we didn't have much luck," one says. "The fishing is probably bad because it's spawning season and the fish have other things on their minds."

We mosey a little further down the trail. Mac stops at the end of the lake to take panoramic pictures of it and the waterfalls. We take our packs off and explore our lake from another angle. A huge fourteen-inch trout faces upstream at the end of the lake where the lake spills into a waterfall.

We load up our packs again. The trail looks different now. I see waterfalls, views, and wildflowers that I didn't see on the way up. I'm not a target of an insect feeding frenzy this time.

We walk. My foot feels strange and really hurts but I don't want to tell Mac. I lace up the boot even tighter. We get comfortable in our packs and find our rhythm.

Soon we meet a man and two young boys. "Is there much snow ahead?" one boy asks.

"Yeah. Lots of snow on the Upper Chain Lake. In fact, the lake is almost all iced over," Mac responds.

They've got quite a walk ahead and it sounds like they've already walked a ways. The man's fair skin looks sunburned. One boy's face is covered in red bumps. I show him the bumps on my forehead. We talk mosquitoes. The other boy, probably ten or eleven years old, is bump free and proud of it.

"We're going home a day early," says the boy without the bumps.

I suspect it's because of the mosquitoes.

"You're so lucky you don't get bit," I say to him. "Maybe you should donate yourself to scientific research." I hope he can tell that I am kidding.

"No way," he says without hesitation.

We say our good-byes and wish each other luck.

I hit the rhythm of my pack and the trail again. Whenever I hit that rhythm, my mind wanders and new ideas come in. I start thinking again about *The Sierra Garden Tour.* I desire to leave the confines of the marked trail, set off cross-country and go in whichever direction my little heart desires. *The 2 oz. Backpacker* says, " . . . true wilderness does not begin until the trail is left behind. . . ."

The Sierra Nevada Mountain Range is a big place. Maybe I could do one section per season. I could spend late spring to early fall in one section of the Sierra at a time. For example, next spring I could take off with a map of Kings Canyon National Park or the Emigrant Wilderness or John Muir Wilderness and live out there all season, backpacking and taking pictures of those breathtaking scenes and moments that I find. I can see it. Man can't create gardens as beautiful and perfect as the ones I have seen out here in the wilds. The Sierra is far too vast for one book. *The Sierra Garden Tour — Dinkey Lakes Wilderness*, by Ellen Pendleton. One season, one area, one book. This project could take the rest of my life. How many different areas are in the Sierra?

The fantasy occupies and amuses my mind and spirit while my body hikes. Going back to "civilization" feels sad. I wish I could stay out here.

When we reach the roadhead, Sandy's car is gone. He beat us in and he beat us out. I hope he found what he was looking for. I hope he had a great time.

The view back is different from the parking area now that we've been out there. We identify Gale Peak. Mac takes panoramic photos of the skyline for further reference. I want them for my memory.

I can't wait to go back, . . . back to the wildness.

August 7, Monday ◯ ♐
A Lesson

The only thing that's going to help me today is tomorrow.
— Sheryl Brookes

I'm reminded to say a word about the little voices we hear inside. I am sitting here today back home and my foot really hurts. At Chain Lakes, when I picked up my heavy pack to move our campsite, That Little Voice told me to put on my boots. My ego snubbed the advice as unnecessary. I ignored That Little Voice. Now I feel very stupid for not listening to That Wise Little Voice that, if I had acted upon, probably would have avoided this pain and debilitating condition. I'm sitting here, immobilized, with my right foot soaking in a hot herbal bath. The injury is not serious, I sense. No bruises with only slight swelling. But my sense is to stay off of it and soak it. I don't want to go to a doctor who, for a fee, will tell me to stay off of it and soak it.

Confidence is a term used to describe those folks who have learned to listen, trust, and act upon their inner voice. Call it intellect, experience, the Higher Self, intuition, common sense, whatever, . . . That Little Voice. Some of the voices we hear are programming received from parents, teachers, friends, society, etc. Some voices are the untethered ego. Sometimes the voice is triggered from a past experience. The trick is to learn which voice to listen to, which voice is the most trustworthy, which voices inhibit independence, and which voice helps. It's taken a long time to learn to listen and choose which voice to trust. It's a *which* hunt. Obviously I'm still learning.

August 8, Tuesday ◯ Capricorn ♑
The Sierra Nevada Mountain Range

Northern Sierra
    Wilderness: Bucks Lake Wilderness
                              Desolation Wilderness
                              Granite Chief Wilderness
                              Mount Rose Wilderness

    National Forest: El Dorado National Forest
                              Plumas National Forest
                              Tahoe National Forest

Central Sierra
    Wilderness: Ansel Adams Wilderness
                              Carson-Iceberg Wilderness
                              Dinkey Lakes Wilderness
                              Emigrant Wilderness
                              Hoover Wilderness
                              John Muir Wilderness
                              Kaiser Wilderness
                              Minarets Wilderness
                              Mokelumne Wilderness

National Forest:	Inyo National Forest
	Sierra National Forest
	Stanislaus National Forest
	Toiyabe National Forest
National Park:	Yosemite National Park

Southern Sierra

Wilderness:	Domeland Wilderness
	Golden Trout Wilderness
	Jennie Lakes Wilderness
	Monarch Wilderness
	South Sierra Wilderness
National Forest:	Sequoia National Forest
National Park:	Kings Canyon National Park
	Sequoia National Park

Reality

I want to know God's thoughts, . . . the rest are details.
— Albert Einstein

What is my purpose on Earth? Perhaps if each of us knew that answer and lived it, we might know harmony here on Earth. Maybe this is harmony? Maybe we are living our purposes by doing exactly what we're doing?

I like Einstein's goal: . . . *to know the thoughts of God.* The Divine Father is the quintessential role model. How better to get to know the Master than to live in the natural world that He created?

I suppose I could use my imagination and fictionalize *The Sierra Garden Tour* experience, rather than physically do it, but I prefer reality. I prefer hands on experiences that contribute to my knowing. Vicarious experiences intrigue and inspire me but do not satisfy me. Real experiences usually include unexpected events; things that I could never imagine might happen. The Universe is full of surprises, . . . delightful surprises. That's what makes life on Earth an adventure. If we insulate ourselves in the human-made world, surprises are limited. But if we become a part of nature again, that's when magic happens.

Perhaps part of our reason on Earth is to learn how to live with other people?

Naw.

Maybe we're here to learn to live with our Self.

PART V — *Journals*

August 13, Sunday ☺ Pisces ♓
Caffeine

Only Irish coffee provides in a single glass all four essential food groups: alcohol, caffeine, sugar, and fat.

— Alex Levine

I love the smell of coffee. But it has come to me that I should stop consuming caffeine. This morning I was trying to meditate and became aware of a "caffeine frequency" or "high" that inhibits, or interferes, with my ability to relax. I have a love/hate relationship with coffee. I've quit many times over the past twenty years and re-started just as many times. Beginning again after a long abstention is almost a hallucinatory experience. Perhaps subconsciously I quit occasionally just so I can experience that initial caffeine rush again. Sometimes my decision to start again was triggered by sadness. I don't like feeling down and at those times, I know a cup of coffee will send me flying. I surrender.

However, after resuming my daily morning cup or two of coffee for any length of time, the excitement dwindles and the morning coffee becomes more like a requirement rather than a spiritual revelation. When I'm a regular coffee drinker, I usually get up in the morning incapable of doing or saying anything, except for random, audible grunts, until I get my morning brew. Only then do I become user friendly.

My reasons for resuming my caffeine intake after a hiatus vary. My reason for quitting is always the same: I sense that caffeine is not good for me. It feels like it is bad for my body. It makes my stomach hurt. And I cannot meditate when I am doing caffeine. So today I've decided to stop, . . . again.

When my first two children were young (birth to five years old) I wouldn't get much time to myself, being a full-time mom. So once a month or whenever the whim hit me, I'd drink a cup or two of coffee after the kids went to bed and I'd stay up all night doing whatever I couldn't do while they were awake, like sew or read. I was not good for much the following day but to me, that time alone was worth the self-abuse. I absolutely LOVE my children and I also enjoy my alone time.

When going cold turkey off caffeine the symptoms usually begin within 24 hours. Incredible headaches move in that can last a week. I've learned to wean off caffeine using half-decaf blends to slowly eliminate the poisonous addiction from my body. I have found it best to wean according to the amount of caffeine in the products, high to low: Coffee, yerba maté, black tea, green tea, white tea, decaf coffee, decaf green tea, then done. Unfortunately, I *love* the taste and smell of coffee.

Once, after a couple of weeks in detox, I experienced lower backache, located around the kidney area. Good-bye caffeine. This writing shall become a landmark on that journey.

From *The Concise Columbia Encyclopedia:*

Caffeine — *odorless, slightly bitter ALKALOID found in coffee, tea, COLA nuts, maté, and COCOA (see CACAO). In moderation, caffeine is a mild stimulant that increases urination and the heart rate and rhythm. Excessive intake can cause restlessness, insomnia, heart irregularities, and delirium.*

Then I look up ALKALOID:

Any class of organic compounds composed of carbon, hydrogen, nitrogen, and usually oxygen that are often derived from plants.

[Sounds harmless so far.]

The name means **alkali like***, but some alkaloids do not exhibit alkaline properties. Many alkaloids, though poisons, have physiological effects that render them valuable as medicines. For example, curarine, found in the deadly extract CURARE, is a powerful muscle relaxant; atropine is used to dilate the pupils of the eye; and physostigmine is used specifically for certain muscular diseases. Narcotic alkaloids used in medicine include MORPHINE and CODEINE for pain relief and COCAINE as a local anesthetic. Other common alkaloids include CAFFEINE, LSD, QUININE, SEROTONIN, STRYCHNINE, and NICOTINE.*

Excuse me? Caffeine is put into the same category as morphine, codeine, LSD, strychnine and nicotine? It is a stimulant, a classified psychoactive/psychotropic drug.

I'm reminded of an interesting observation. Years ago I attended a concert at Esalen Institute in Big Sur, California, a benefit for SEVA Foundation. Bonnie Raitt, Jackson Brown, and Kenny Loggins performed. The daytime event was non-alcoholic. Fortunately I was in a caffeine and alcohol abstention phase. What I observed was that at about 3:30 p.m. the line to the cappuccino/espresso cart was incredibly long and growing longer. Since alcohol was not allowed, these folks required something to alter their minds and bodies. They were willing to stand in the coffee line that was more than ten times longer than the lines to the port-a-potties. The event helped me realize how powerful and widespread caffeine, *the legal drug,* has become.

August 14, Monday ☽ ♈
More Caffeine

The Caffeine Book: A User's and Abuser's Guide by Frances Sheridan Goulart. I found it at the library between one book titled in large red type, COCAINE and another book titled HEROIN. I nudged a lady in the aisle close to me and said, "Look at this. I just want to show this to someone."

This is Day Three Detox. I have had some decaf coffee. The package I opened this morning read, "99.7% caffeine free." Tonight I have a slight neck ache, but surprisingly, so far so good. I was drinking two cups maximum every morning and at home we make half decaf with half regular anyway, so maybe I don't have so far to fall.

The Caffeine Book is remarkable. It says we live in a country where "80% of us drink coffee. That includes 50% of all Americans over the age of 10, and 83% of the medical profession." This book more than convinces me that caffeine is a drug that I will live without. Coffee grounds do help create excellent garden compost, however. I'm only on page 25 of the book but my love affair with coffee is over. I have been deceived, falling for the marketing ploy. It is not a harmless beverage but rather an addictive drug with long term effects that we have come to accept as part of the human natural aging process. I choose not to be addicted. I choose freedom. I choose health.

> "Coffee would not be approved today if it were being presented to the Federal Food and Drug Administration for consideration. Once tests of it were completed and all of the side effects honestly evaluated, it would probably be confined to a doctor's prescription only," writes Ray Josephs in *Nutrition Health Review*.
>
> — from *The Caffeine Book*

Do twelve step programs exist for caffeine addicts?

August 19, Saturday ◯ ♊

Mac leaves today on his annual backpack trip with the boys. I want to go so badly that I feel goofy.

August 20, Sunday ◯ *void of course* (v/c)
Patience

And that, I guess, is quite a lot to get out of such a simple thing as walking.
> — Colin Fletcher, *The Complete Walker III*

I will bless every day that I'm able to get out of bed and walk again without pain. It's been two weeks since I hurt my foot backpacking and I'm still not up to speed. My heart and soul would love to pull on those hiking boots right now and go for just a little walk. Maybe I should try? My foot isn't in much pain, so maybe some exercise might strengthen it. I could walk the mile or so to and from the corner store where I buy my lottery ticket.

I set out but only make it a few blocks before shooting pain stops me. Slowly, so slowly, I walk back toward home, knowing cars are cursing me as I limp through the crosswalk. I walk so slowly, wondering if I should call someone for a ride home. How frustrating and foolish is this? If I knew that this was a lifetime condition, I would probably resign myself to learn and live with it. But I know that it's going to heal and that I will walk with ease again. I thought today was the day. It might be a cracked bone; I just have to be patient and let it heal. (Doctors *practice* and we're *patient*.)

I stop a few more times, make it home and will never again take for granted "such a simple thing as walking." Perhaps the Universe gave me this lesson to help me appreciate the gifts I have been given. I will look at people in wheelchairs differently now. I will look at people walking slowly, so slowly, differently now. I am thankful and grateful for this new insight allowing me to empathize with others. And I further appreciate the gift of good health more than I did two weeks ago. Perhaps I can learn patience too.

With lots of time to think of walking, I do Colin's astrological aspects and compare them with mine. I can't decipher his ascendant, (rising sign), without his actual birth time and I don't have it. Without the birth time I can't figure out the houses. But I can get a general feeling. He was born March 14, 1922:

	Colin Fletcher	me
☼ Sun	♓ Pisces	♓ Pisces
Ascendant		♐ Sagittarius
☽ Moon	♎ Libra	♌ Leo
Mercury	♒ Aquarius	♈ Aries
Venus	♈ Aries	♒ Aquarius
Mars	♐ Sagittarius	♏ Scorpio
Jupiter	♎ Libra	♈ Aries
Saturn	♎ Libra	♎ Libra
Uranus	♓ Pisces	♋ Cancer
Neptune	♌ Leo	♎ Libra
Pluto	♋ Cancer	♌ Leo
fire	3	5
water	3	3
air	4	3
earth	0	0
mutable	3	2
cardinal	5	5
fixed	2	4

His signature is cardinal/air = Libra
My signature is cardinal/fire = Aries
(opposite on the zodiac)

Also, 1922 was the year of the Dog in Chinese astrology.
I'm opposite, the year of the Dragon. Interesting.

Noting the similarities, I draw lines from Libra to
Libra, Aries to Aries, etc. Wouldn't it be curious if his rising
sign was Scorpio? That's the only sign missing from his
chart compared with mine. Neither chart has any earth
signs. I must find out what time he was born, if he knows.

So I feel that looking at him is like looking at my
mirror male counterpart. I'm being presumptuous and
flattering my Self to say that we're so much alike but I feel it
is so. Of course differences exist; no two daisies are exactly
alike. I wish I could spend more time with him. I feel I

could learn a lot about myself by being with him. I feel he could find a dear friend in me. Can we ever have too many dear friends?

This foot injury offers plenty of down time to read and contemplate, plenty of time to give thanks for all the good in my life, plenty of time to think of all the things I could do if my foot didn't hurt. In the millennium of all time, two weeks is but a flip of an eyelash. But in my time, every moment is precious. Two weeks is as long as the present moment, now, that is neither past nor future but timeless.

As I sit soaking my foot in an Epsom salt bath, I feel impatient and eager to be well. I can't wait until I can painlessly and effortlessly scramble up the rocks to catch a view. I can't wait to carry my backpack again or at least take a simple walk. This is yet another lesson in patience. Enough lessons, already. Do they ever stop coming?

It's important to remember how lucky I am and to give thanks. *Dear God, let me get up each morning and give thanks for my good health. Let me always remember how good it feels to walk on two healthy feet. Let my children, Mac, my friends and my family always be healthy and happy.*

August 24, Thursday ☼ ♍ / ◯ ♌
Update

I can walk today without a limp and without pain. Oh joy!

Mac is scheduled to come home from the wilderness tonight. Barb (John's wife) calls this afternoon to find out if I'd heard from them yet. John called her yesterday from somewhere on the road. She tells me that while they were out backpacking it rained for three hours straight and the mosquitoes were gruesome. They packed out yesterday and were planning on car camping last night and fishing today. She said they'd be home some time today. I can't wait to hear Mac's stories. I hope he took lots of pictures.

September 2, Saturday ☉ ♐

My foot is still not healed completely. I really think that I must have broken or cracked a bone. I've been wearing a neoprene elbow brace on it that helps. My hiking boots have the best support when laced up tight. I'm feeling frustrated not being able to go hiking. It's Labor Day weekend and I'd love to go camping and hiking. My appreciation of good health has elevated.

Learning to Meditate

Interestingly enough, I have unconsciously and instinctively, from the very beginning, adopted the practices used by initiates in meditation.
— Edgar Cayce, *Edgar Cayce on ESP*

I heard in a lecture once that the only way to learn Transcendental Meditation is from a master. My question was, "Who taught the Master?"

I meditate. I transcend my lower self to my Higher Self and learned "by accident." It happened years ago, while I attended a conference sponsored by the company for which I worked. The event was held in Oakland, California, in a tall hotel overlooking a section of the Nimitz Freeway damaged in the Loma Prieta Earthquake, October 17, 1989.

This is from my journal at that time:

We arrive at the hotel in the early afternoon after a two-hour drive. We check into our rooms and immediately go to the opening ceremonies and classes. Our sales-oriented company fills the convention center with high motivational energy. We take a break at 5:30 p.m. The Awards Banquet is scheduled for 7 p.m., a formal affair where many of the women will be dressed to the "T" in their sequined and beaded gowns. The anticipation mounts.

I'm sharing the hotel room with my friend and sister consultant, Aiko, a special person whose delightful character warrants an entire chapter of her own. Our room is on the 19th floor, facing west, overlooking the damaged section of the Nimitz Freeway, that is still closed to repair damages. I return to the room. Aiko stays downstairs to eat dinner. I have about an hour to shower, fluff, dress, and meet my director downstairs.

As I view the spectacular sunset over the San Francisco skyline, I am painfully aware of an acquired stress headache. The two-hour drive in traffic, the excitement, the seminar info input, etc., has saturated and overloaded my brain capacity. As I stare out of the window and soak in the beauty, my mood becomes marred by fear. *What if we have another earthquake? I'm up here on the 19th floor. If the building starts to crumble, should I run to the door? go to the window? hang onto the plumbing? What should I do?* I read the room door for evacuation procedures and walk down the hallway to familiarize myself with the stairway exits. I take a deep breath.

Going back into the room the sunlight shining on the bed immediately catches my attention. *Maybe a little nap would help.* I take off my shoes, spread my body out on the bed to soak up the warmth of the sunlight. I feel like a cat and begin to relax. Thoughts of an earthquake again fill my brain. Fear impedes my comfort. Internal conversations concerning evacuation scenarios plague my thoughts. I become almost hysterical. The sun continues to give me its beautiful, warm light.

Then I realize that in order to relax, I must get rid of this feeling of fear. This doesn't seem like an easy task. I begin by thinking of other things. Then the internal conversation shifts back, *This building survived the Loma Prieta Earthquake. Everything will be all right.* The fear melts and I begin to relax. I slide into the space between wakefulness and sleep, a magical gap that suspends the doer. I slip over to the other side into slumber.

No sooner do I surrender to sleep, than the phone rings. I pop up. It's my director, Skye. She's the motherly type. She wants to make sure that I have found my room and that everything is all right.

When we hang up I attempt to pick up where I left off in mid-nap. The sun's warmth feels so good. Surprisingly, part of my headache has gone away. Then more fears come to mind: *I hope the kids are okay. I hope I don't fall asleep and won't be late for the banquet. I hope I'll look okay tonight. I hope I don't fall up or down the stairs when I cross the stage.* The thoughts ramble on until I realize that I'm not going to fall asleep again until these thoughts shut up. So I focus on the warmth of the sunlight and the comfort of the bed. Soon, I drift again into that place between wakefulness and sleep. A dance of light fills my awareness and I enjoy the show. Thoughts creep in and immediately the dance stops. I focus on the light, . . . and, . . . slip away. . . .

Ring . . . ring . . . .

Again? I pop up and answer the phone, "Hello?"

It's Skye again. She forgot to give me her room number.

I thank her, then sit, feeling somewhat light-headed and funny. More of my headache has disappeared! There remains still that little bit, so, for a third time I return to my catnap.

I know that I have to get any thoughts out of the way. I know that I have to forget about my body. I linger longer in that space between wake and sleep, watching the lightshow, fascinated, and in wonder. And then without notice, I slip away.

Ring . . . ring . . . .

Again? What are the chances? I answer.

Skye again, confirming our meeting time and place.

I cheerfully thank her and hang up completely aware that the headache is now gone. I breathe deeply and smile. I feel great!

I shower and fluff. Later I walk across the stage without falling and have a wonderful evening.

Since that experience it has become my research project "to practice falling asleep." Cats are great role models. Mac is the Nap Master. They are my teachers.

I have become intrigued with the lightshow. The colors vary from a light blue to a deep indigo, sometimes violet. The lights pulsate, like drops of water creating circular, rippling waves on water. When I am treated to the lightshow, I know that I'm "there" in that special state. The more intense the state, the clearer the picture and the deeper the colors. Sometimes a golden-white circle appears around the ripples. I explore this new addition. *Is it new or have I just become aware of it?* Occasionally I see something small and distant sitting in the middle of the sphere of light.

I used to feel embarrassed to announce to the family, "Excuse me. I'm going to go meditate." So I've learned to tell them, "I'm going to go and rest my eyes," or "I'm going to take a nap." I know they won't tease me about that. I don't meditate sitting in the traditional lotus position. I can, but I'm aware of the energy that it takes to remain upright. I prefer lying down on my back. I can't sleep on my back, so this position keeps me awake. Also, if I do by chance slip into the sleep state, I usually give a little snort that wakes me up. Mac gets a big kick out of this. Occasionally it's not my snort that wakes me up but rather his laughter. However it works, I enjoy lying down to meditate.

One afternoon, years ago, Aja and I were out in the car doing errands. She was probably eight or nine years old. The summer day was warm and sunny, (unusual for where we live on the Monterey Peninsula). At 3:30 p.m. I pull over and park. We're on Garden Road, a lovely wooded business area near the airport. Aja asks, "What are you doing?"

"I'm going to take a little nap."

She looks at me and wrinkles her brow, "Here?"

"It's time. We'll be fine," I assure her.

"Well there's no way I can take a nap," she states in no uncertain terms indicating that she is just too old for such nonsense. She attempts to talk me out of it but I tell her that I just need a few minutes to rest my eyes. I offer her a pillow but she scoffs at it and almost pouts.

"Can't we just go?" Persistence is her virtue.

My stubbornness wins. Besides, I have the car keys. I proceed to get comfortable, enjoying the warmth of the sun beaming through the car windows. I move the car to take full advantage of the sunlight. Within minutes I calm down and enter that wondrous place of peace between wakefulness and sleep.

When I emerge, I feel great, refreshed. The brush with sleep released all the tension that had accumulated. I glance over to behold the funniest sight: Aja sits, mouth open, head back, snoring loudly and drooling down her chin. My laughter wakes her up. "Are you ready to go?" I ask.

Without a word she takes the pillow, climbs into the back seat, and resumes her slumberfest for another hour. She'll hate my telling this but it was just too funny to skip. Children know how to meditate.

A few notes: I've found it best to meditate on an empty stomach. I like to leave at least an hour after eating, preferably two. I like to meditate before eating in the morning. I like 3:30 p.m. with the afternoon sun shining on the bed. Meditating in natural surroundings is especially joyful.

The most intense visual lightshow I ever experienced occurred on a camping trip at Huntington Lake in the Sierra:

114

I zip the tent so the bugs won't bother me and then lie down. With eyes closed I instantly become aware of the multitude of birdsongs that fills the woods. It sounds like they are talking with each other. I hear songs that I've never heard before. I slip away. Suddenly I'm surprised by something inside my circle of light. I focus and give it all of my attention. It seems far away, like in a tunnel. I struggle and squint to catch a better look. I see what appears to be someone sitting, far, far away, . . . sitting on a rock or something. Someone surrounded by beautifully intense colors – blues, purples, white, and gold. I *try* to, . . . *poof*. . . . It disappears.

Curiosity. Joy. Empty. Longing. What was that? Come back. Who are you? Was it a fluke . . . a coincidence? Maybe the birdsongs set the scene? Maybe the altitude contributes to the intensity of meditating, . . . maybe the lighter air, . . . maybe being closer to "heaven", . . . the Himalayas. Is this why people find themselves obsessed with mountains and the high country? I long to experience that vision again.

Upon returning home, I first hear the mockingbirds. Then I hear seagulls, jays, and an occasional hawk. How strange a city must look to a hawk.

I began to meditate regularly after reading *The Autobiography of a Yogi*, by Paramahansa Yogananda. He describes and confirms the lightshow that I see, so I figure I'm on the right track. I still have much to learn but I've decided that meditation is vital to the spirit. When we eat and exercise we give attention to the body. When we read and think we give attention to the mind. When we meditate we give all of our attention to our soul, our Higher Self, our spirit. We're spending time alone with our spirit and with God. We must get to the place where we trust our Body; trust that it'll be okay until we return to consciousness. We have to trust our environment; trust that our Body will be safe until we return to consciousness. The act of reaching that level of trust facilitates a vibration of the Human Form that allows the opportunity to give complete attention to one's Higher Self, the spirit, the SoulBody, that connection with God. Trust is a high frequency on the human energetic scale and brings peace. I've found the act of meditating to be a necessary part of my daily life and feel that it is cumulative. We get better at it the more we do it. We get in shape. I like to meditate three times a day, a minimum of two, and it's a shame if I can only do it once.

"But I don't have time," friends say. When I realized the importance of meditation, I began to make the time. We all have time to spend loving our Selves, if we make it a priority. I believe that we are, in essence, spirit. We have decided to come to Earth to gather experience, enjoy ourselves and, through awareness and attention, evolve our level of consciousness and be spirit on Earth. We live here, learning to love ourselves and others. Our spirit created our body, our mind, our personality, and our ego as tools to be used for our spiritual growth. We forget this. Our personalities and egos have the ability to take off by themselves, and sometimes in opposite directions.

When we spend time with our Self, we cultivate and nurture our soul. Things become very clear. The soul becomes stronger and peaceful. It regains the connection and trust of the Higher Self and the Universe. When I meditate regularly I find myself smiling unconditionally at people, smiling without thoughts or judgments. I find myself happier and less concerned with troubles. I find myself having more love to give.

Timing is everything. When I was just out of high school, a friend gave me Yogananda's book and said, "Here, I think you'll enjoy this." I started reading it then but just couldn't get into it. Life moved on. I grew. I changed. I lived. Years ago, the book kept popping into my awareness. I'd go to a friend's house, it'd be on the coffee table. I'd talk to a friend on the telephone, she'd have it sitting on the table next to her. "Coincidence is God's way of remaining anonymous." Things seem to come in threes for me, so when I saw the book sitting on the seat next to my good friend Corina in her car, I said out loud, "Okay, I'll read the book." So timing is everything and the time comes when the time comes. Enjoy the process.

Meditation, then, is bringing the mind home.
— Sogyal Rinpoche

PART VI — *Sierra Garden Tour Revisited*

September 2, Saturday ☽ ♐
Obsessed

One should go to the woods for safety, if for nothing else.
　　　　　　　—John Muir, *Our National Parks*

We go to a party. I step gingerly, still feeling vulnerable regarding my foot injury. I chat with a local Forest Service ranger. We've talked previously about the Sierra Nevada at another dinner party. He was born and raised on the eastern Sierra. He lived there through the early years of his marriage but then boredom hit his wife. She evidently didn't like having to drive fifty miles to go to a "good" shopping mall. So he, his wife and son moved away from his beloved Sierra.

　　As we talk I tell him stories of my recent backpack trips. We are both tickled to find someone else who likes to talk about being *out there*. We talk about mosquitoes, birds, ecology, the Forest Service, all kinds of fun things. He feels and knows my excitement, "You've got it. You've got the bug," and recommends the book *Silent Spring* by Rachel Carson.

I also talk to another friend, Steve, who has always seemed quite deep but we have never stopped to share much conversation. Maybe it's the wine tonight but he opens up. He reveals that when he was a child, he would go camping with his family. Every morning he would set his alarm for 5:30 a.m., get up, and be gone until late afternoon. He would spend the days listening to the wind in the trees, fishing and just being with nature. He would bring fish back to camp to help justify his solo outings. He tells me, "I need nature but could easily live without people." His inner silence comes from nature.

I understand.

So I go to parties and talk about being *out there*. I write about being *out there* and complain about not being able to go *out there*. I am restless, obsessed, and homesick.

September 7, Thursday ◯ Aquarius ♒
Pisces

My mind is my own church.
— Thomas Paine

Well. So. Are you going to stick your big toe across that thick imaginary line, or are you not? Will you risk confrontation in order to scratch that itch in your ambition, or will you instead shuffle back to your comfort zone and endlessly replay your itchy daydreams? I'm sure you can tell I'm rooting for you to pull off the first possibility, i.e. do what you fear. But that doesn't mean you should. Whatever bold move you make this week, you should make sure you're not trying to impress me or anyone else. Do it to prove you respect yourself, or don't do it.
—Rob Brezsny, *FreeWillAstrology*, August 24-30

I surround myself with pictures, videos, maps and guidebooks of the Sierra. I blatantly complain about my immobility resulting from my foot injury. If I won the lottery today, I would go backpacking in the Sierra as soon as my foot is well.

I read the above newspaper horoscope and describe to Mac and Sunshine my dream of *The Sierra Garden Tour*. This confession might be the "confrontation" indicated in the horoscope. I anticipate being greeted with a barrage of practical reasons why this dream won't work.

And yes, they give plenty of reasons why this will not work. But they also offer advice on getting started. Mac keeps saying, "there are so many wildflower books already." Yes, they agree that if I start now maybe I could make progress by the end of my lifetime. They don't respond as negatively as I thought they would. They are being helpful and practical. I'm a dreamer. But I had to take a chance and say something to them; I took a risk, exposed my daydreams and now I can move on.

I feel vulnerable letting Mac know that I'm an insatiable dreamer. I'm feeling irresponsible sharing with my daughter that suddenly I want to go backpacking and spend seasons out there in hopes of producing a book on the gardens of the wild world.

This occupies my mind and I could try to defuse the restlessness. This desire and obsession to be *out there* may be equated with the restless desire of the soul to live in God's world. Nature — God. Perhaps I have been neglecting my spiritual practices too much. Perhaps I should discipline myself to meditate more. Perhaps I should resume my studies with the Self-Realization Fellowship. Perhaps the desire I feel is the desire to be nearer to God. Perhaps that's the bell that rings when we're *out there* in nature that reminds us of who we are and what we're doing on Earth. Young Yogananda was always trying to escape to the Himalayas to become enlightened. His guru, Sri Yukteswar, advised his student of his folly:

> "Poor boy, mountains cannot give you what you want." Master spoke caressingly, comfortingly. His calm gaze was unfathomable. "Your heart's desire shall be fulfilled."

I'm sensing that what I really want is to become a spiritual Earth being. Upon stating this, my restless feet change to a restless heart, seeking the kingdom of God. The obsession subsides. It is replaced with a calm, peaceful feeling and an awareness that I have much work to do. Is this crazy? Many will say *yes*. But this is my path. The trailhead is accessible to everyone on Earth. You don't need a car, a backpack, food, a sleeping bag or a tent. All you need to get to the destination is within each of us. The joy of the journey is a gift from the Giver of all gifts, God. Life on Earth is our gift from God. Even the most illustrious scientist Albert Einstein knew the importance of communing with the Higher Power. What's good enough for Einstein is certainly good enough for me. Besides, Albert was a Pisces too.

When in doubt, tell the truth.
— Mark Twain

Doubt rears its ugly head as a little voice chimes: *Perhaps I'm adopting this spiritual attitude to avoid doing The Sierra Garden Tour? Perhaps I've created this spiritual focus to avoid the impracticality of my dream.*

The horoscope says, *do what you fear.* That is the key. Do I fear going to the wilderness by myself for any length of time? No. I fear leaving my family alone, even though I know they will be taken care of. Perhaps I fear that they might find out that they can live without me. I fear that my twelve-year-old would worry tremendously about her mother *out there*. I fear losing Mac. I fear being accused of abandoning my responsibilities for the pleasures I might find in the wilderness. Yes there's plenty of fear here in this daydream. Should I do what I fear? Would it be stupid? Or empowering?

The horoscope also says, *Whatever bold move you make this week, you should make sure you're not trying to impress me or anyone else. Do it to prove you respect yourself, or don't do it.* I would do it to prove to myself that a spiritual reality is translatable to practical Earth reality. I've learned not to become attached to the results. So how can spirituality be proved? Can it only be proved to oneself? But the horoscope says, "Do it to prove you *respect* yourself. . . ."

> respect, [< L. *re-*, back + *specere*, look at]
> 1. To feel or show honor or esteem for.
> (*Webster's New World Dictionary*).

So, if I don't believe in my dreams and actively pursue them, they're worthless. Honor my dreams. Honor my spiritualism. Honor thy Self.

I have no doubt that meditation is the pathway to God. I have no doubt that I could do *The Sierra Garden Tour*. The rest are details. I can take the feeling of restless obsession and channel that energy to dedicate my Self to spiritual study and meditation. I shall seek the company of God not only in the wilderness but within my Self and thus find God everywhere. Namaste.

September 8, Friday ☽ ♓

Go away. I'm alright.
　　　　　　— H.G. Wells, his last words

I go swimming at the Monterey Sports Center. I need some exercise and haven't thought about swimming until today. It feels so good. There's no impact or pressure on my foot and I can swim all I want.

September 10, Sunday ○ ♈
Maps

There must be more to life than having everything.
— Maurice Sendak

The maps I ordered arrived yesterday. Oh, how exciting! They're beautiful. I sit and read them for hours.

Deer season opens this weekend in some areas of the Sierra. Do deer hunters pose any danger to backpackers? I hope Mac and I can go on another backpacking trip in the Sierra before the snow falls. I walk now without pain. Oh how I have waited for this day. By next week my foot should feel close to normal. They currently don't allow firearms in National Parks. This is good.

September 15, Friday ○ ♊

Some unwonted, taught pride diverts us from our original intent, which is to explore the neighborhood, view the landscape, to discover at least where it is that we have been so startlingly set down, if we can't learn why.

— Annie Dillard, *Pilgrim at Tinker Creek*

Mac and I walk out of the house and head straight up Jefferson Street to Veterans Memorial Park. My foot does great so far. Once at the park we opt for the trail rather than following the road. This is the first trail since my foot injury.

I feel unsure and timid. I don't trust the foot at all. I'm reluctant to make little jumps and climbs that I wouldn't have thought about before. I'm cautious and slow. We venture into an abandoned quarry by my old junior high school. I've known about the quarry but have never visited. The smoker kids in junior high would cut class and hang out here. I never cut class. I never smoked. I feel a Native American energy here.

We hike for about two hours. I love this. We tromp through bushes and up steep trails. I am so happy to be back out here. I am home. *Thank you for letting my foot heal. Namaste.*

September 18, Monday ☽ ♋
Jack's Peak

Call the trip a "walk," "walking" is fun but "hiking" is work.
— Robert S. Wood, *The 2 oz. Backpacker*

Mac and I spent the weekend at the Monterey Jazz Festival. This year's festival was excellent. A fourth venue opened this year and the hardest part of the festival was trying to see all the performers. So many great musicians were playing at the same time at different locations. I sat in on the press conference with Bobby McFerrin and met him later outside. Amazing dude.

Today is Monday, recovery day. The festival always exhausts me. The weather is lovely. Sunshine has time and expresses a desire to take a walk up to Jack's Peak. I feel the need to clear my mind of all that jazz and get back *out there*. The day is warm and still. September is generally a fine-weathered month here on the Monterey Peninsula. Usually just as soon as school starts, the summer fog is replaced by warm, sunny days. We get in the car and go.

Sunshine and I walk up to the top of Jack's Peak, sit in the sun, shoo the bugs away, view the views, play with a lizard and talk. After a while we loop back and I show her the Monterey vista and display map that sits alongside the trail. The view is spectacular from here.

Heading back to our trail, Sunshine stops suddenly and puts her arm out to stop me.

"Bird," she whispers.

Down our trail a huge bird, standing on the ground, rummages its head between a rock and a bush. Its tail flips from side to side. A big wing stretches out and down. The bird ruffles then out pops its head and looks straight at us. We stand perfectly still. An owl. It looks like a Great Horned Owl because of its size and the horny feathers atop its head. In its mouth, a red and black snake wriggles. The owl stops, looks at us, then shifts all of its attention back onto the snake. It repeats this five or six times until lunch is done. I wonder if it can sense our wonder? After lunch, it takes flight. How lucky are we? We walk on.

"Do you ever fly in your dreams?" I ask.

"Only once. I flew over a river. Flying was great. Easy. I was looking for a little lost child. I did a lot of flying and finally found her. Bears were taking care of her. I flew down, got her and we flew off together."

She gives me a look that tickles my nose and melts my spirit.

Then she continues, "I have a lot of dreams about swimming. I can breathe underwater."

"Wow!"

We walk and talk.

What a lovely day this is.

PART VII — *Autumn*

September 21, Thursday ☉ ♌
Day One, Lone Pine

Any journey is a pilgrimage.
— Paulo Coelho

Mac and I take off for the eastern Sierra. We leave Monterey before sunrise and drive south through Bakersfield, over the Tehachapi Pass, then north on Highway 395. We find Lone Pine Ranger Station in the hot, dry desert with dried up Owens Lake to the east. To the west, climbing quickly to the sky from the flatness of the valley floor, stands the Sierra, majestic and humbling.

At first I can't pick out which one is Mount Whitney. All the peaks are magnificent. Depth of field can play tricks in determining the highest point. Mac has always wanted to climb Mount Whitney, the highest point in the lower 48 United States. The display outside at the Lone Pine ranger station was designed to assist and guide the viewer to discover and identify Mount Whitney. I soon find it. It wasn't the peak that I thought but once I know it, I can see and feel its magnitude. It looks small next to the surrounding peaks but it is further west behind the closer peaks. It becomes unmistakable.

Inside the visitor's center/ranger station we explore the selection of guidebooks, maps, postcards and photographic journals. And there it is, top shelf: *The Sierra Nevada Natural History* book that my friend Genie had brought over one night. I had been looking for it in used bookstores. We buy it along with a lovely book full of gorgeous color photos called *California's Eastern Sierra, A Visitor's Guide* by Sue Irwin. The ranger helps when we ask for guidance toward a good camping spot.

We consult our campground bible, Tom Stienstra's *California Camping: The Complete Guide.* We head first for Tuttle Creek Camp, a no fee spot along Horseshoe Meadow Road. It is available for Whitney climbers overflow camping. Stienstra rates it 4 on a scale of 10. Trees are scarce; it's flat and uneventful but free. It is Thursday and we see many empty campsites.

We drive back to Whitney Portal Road. Lone Pine Campground, elevation 6,000 feet, nestles in close on the lap of Lone Pine Peak and the road to Whitney Portal. Stienstra rates it an 8. Trees, Lone Pine Creek, seclusion, vacancies and a spectacular view of Mount Whitney. We are home.

I set up the tent while Mac takes care of the site paperwork and gets some firewood from the camp host. I line up the tent door to face east. We set up camp, build a fire, cook and eat dinner while the sun sets behind Mount Whitney. After cleaning up, we read by lantern glow, discuss the next day's plans and watch the starry night sky unveil its glory.

September 22, Friday ☽ ♍
Day Two, Cottonwood Lakes

I sleep well, warm and comfortable with my sleeping bag unzipped.

Suddenly I wake and unzip the tent door. It's the first morning light and a tiny sliver of a crescent moon hovers near the morning glow. It's a magical morning. I quickly dress and go outside to play. It is still dark enough to use my flashlight. To my surprise, other campers are up and moving about. Perhaps they are going to climb Mount Whitney today. The guidebooks recommend starting at the first light if you plan to hike the 22-mile round trip to the summit and back in one day. Some guidebooks recommend earlier, like 3 or 4 a.m. We don't plan on doing this. The elevation gain is approximately 6,100 feet. No, this will not happen today.

With camera in hand I walk toward higher ground, up, up, up, looking for a good spot. Morning magic happens. I don't see any critters. The morning light offers photos not available at any other time of the day. Mount Whitney captures the first pink light. Then the other peaks catch it and the color drips down. I savor the silence, enjoy the peace, respect the process and admire the beauty. Rather than feeling alone, I feel intimate and a part of the Earth. I feel lucky to be awake at this moment and in this enchantingly beautiful place. I feel privy to something special as I watch this part of Planet Earth wake up.

Eager to get on with the day, I go back to camp and begin boiling water for Mac's morning coffee. *How could he sleep at a time like this?* I quietly busy myself with other things, letting him sleep for a while. I sit and meditate in the morning sun. Life is good.

Like a child waiting for Christmas, I make his coffee. Since I don't drink coffee any more, I bought a new single-cup filter especially for backpacking and camping and I am eager to use it. I take the cup of coffee to the tent and urge him to get up. He resists but I nag until he has at least two gulps of brew to jumpstart his system.

After a leisurely breakfast we make plans. We'll drive up to Horseshoe Meadows, some twenty miles away, and dayhike to the Cottonwood Lakes area. We'll camp here another night. Mac takes care of the paperwork, I take care of the dishes. Yes! Hot water and bubbles!

We drive south on Horseshoe Meadows Road for a couple of miles then the road begins to ascend. Up, up. On the map, I count six major switchbacks to reach the top of the first climb. From then we'll drive westward, up then down.

I ask Mac to stop occasionally so I can attempt to acclimate and hopefully prevent altitude sickness. He does so without question or complaint. The view of Owens Valley and the mostly dried up Owens Lake from the heights is vast and gorgeous. I don't think Mac minds the occasional stop. He takes photos. I drink a lot of water and attempt to identify a flowering yellow bush that grows everywhere along the roadside. *Golden Fleece*, I settle on. *The Sierra Nevada Natural History* book covers the flora and fauna of the Sierra with many illustrations, photos and informative explanations that help educate the reader. What a gem of a book it is. Cars should come equipped with a bookshelf.

Up and over we pass next to Wonoga Peak overlooking a lovely green valley lined with pine trees. This is such a contrast from the hot desert below where we were just minutes ago. This will be my first big walk since my foot injury. Mac wisely opted for us not to go backpacking yet. The backpack weight could prove to be too much too soon. This'll be a trial run (or walk).

Elevation at the trailhead to Cottonwood Lakes is about 10,000 feet. This spot would be great for folks who can't or don't want to hike or backpack but would like to experience the Sierra High Country, as much as can be done this close to a road.

Trailhead for Cottonwood Lakes is in the Golden Trout Wilderness and after walking north a little more than two miles, we enter the John Muir Wilderness. Perhaps it's a fact or perhaps it is my imagination but as soon as we pass the John Muir Wilderness sign everything becomes more beautiful. The trees become gnarled and twisted with character, age and wisdom.

Mac and I hike in about six miles and discover many picturesque alpine lakes. To the flowers it is springtime up here. We hike up to Old Army Pass. A lovely, but I'm sure frigid, alpine lake nestles in the lap of the pass. It's Cottonwood Lake #5 or #6. Somebody has set up camp close by. I hope we can come back to this region and camp some day. It is gorgeous up here.

On the way back to the car Mac becomes *barn sour* (a term used to describe a horse that speeds up the pace on the journey home as it senses the barn). Mac breaks into a gallop. I feel no problem with my foot. I am feeling rather tired and out of shape and have a slight headache. Mac runs ahead and I let him go. He passes a number of other hikers.

Back at the car we cruise Horseshoe Meadow parking lot, although we can't see much from the car. Colorful tents hide under trees and it feels like a great campground. To hike from here to Mount Whitney summit, going around to the northwest of here, is about 38.5 miles, according to the indispensable guidebook *California Hiking* by Tom Stienstra and Michael Hodgson. That'd be a nice walk. Three, four, five days?

We drive back down to our camp at Lone Pine Campground. Everything is still intact, although the number of fellow campers has increased to near capacity. It *is* Friday night after all. We drive into town to get ice, food and beer.

We get back to our campsite after dark, so I cook dinner by the light of our lantern. We have a lovely dinner and sit around the fire talking. As I prepare for bed, I put in my order to get up early enough to catch the sunrise again. New moon is on Sunday, so there should be a baby moon on the horizon at sunrise tomorrow but none on Sunday.

I don't sleep well, afraid that I might not wake up in time for the break of dawn. I wake up throughout the night, unzip the tent and peek to see if it is time to get up. Finally I fall into a deep sleep.

September 23, Saturday ☼ Libra ♎ / ◯ ♍
Day Three, Mount Whitney

I unzip the tent. YES! There it is: The morning light. Oh what a treat. But where's the moon? It should be on the horizon near where the sun will rise. I get up, get dressed and grab my flashlight. It's still dark, so I'm just in time.

I walk away from the tent and look back, east toward the Inyo Mountains. As I watch, the baby moon pops up over the dark peaks. *Oh how beautiful. How lucky am I? Thank you.*

I grab the camera and head off to higher land. The Lone Pine campground is down near a creek bed, so up I go. It's not far but what a difference going up makes in visibility. A 4½-mile trail goes up from here to Whitney Portal. *They* say it's best to catch a ride up to portal and walk down the trail. *They* say it's incredibly gorgeous with waterfalls and lush pine forests. Some say it's more beautiful than the trail from Whitney Portal up but I find that hard to believe.

I walk, getting closer to the mountains. The Eastern Sierra is so different from the western side. The western foothills appear gradually and climb gently becoming mountain peaks, moving into the high country. On the eastern side, at least here in Lone Pine, sprawls the flat, massive Owens Valley desert. The desert spreads west, closer to the mountains, still flat but ascending slightly. Desert, desert, desert, then BAM, . . . suddenly, straight-up mountains appear. The Mount Whitney summit is easily visible from here, now that I know what it looks like.

I follow the trail closer to the base of Lone Pine Peak. The top tip of Mount Whitney turns a soft pink. Quickly it lights up into an intense pink, then almost red. I snap pictures, wondering if the camera can possibly capture the intense colors that I see. The light moves down the mountainsides like paint dripping from above, slowly dribbling downward. The pink flows down, closer, . . . closer. The sun peeks over the horizon and daytime happens quickly. I'm thankful that I didn't miss this. I feel very lucky to be here now.

I adventure on, knowing Mac isn't up yet. The campers below come alive. It looks as though every campsite is occupied.

When I return to our "home," (campsite #22), Mac is still snoozing. I get the breakfast cooking hardware ready to rip and start heating the water for tea and coffee. I sit enjoying the morning sun and meditate.

After a leisurely breakfast we pack it up and drive up to Whitney Portal. Our campground, elevation 6,000 feet, is seven miles west of the city of Lone Pine, elevation 3,710 feet. Whitney Portal, elevation 8,360 feet, is 13 miles west of Lone Pine, another six miles up the road from the campground. Up, up, up. The canyon is beautiful. Little ranger cabins, waterfalls, and pine trees line the canyon and the walking trail follows Lone Pine Creek. Cars sit parked alongside the road for at least a half-a-mile from the trailhead at portal. I hope we can find parking up there.

We reach the portal, follow the traffic signs and find an empty space right next to a roaring waterfall. We give thanks to the Parking Angel. When we get out of the car, the air temperature is quite cool, perhaps because of the air conditioning effect of the cold waterfall or perhaps from the altitude gain. The waterfall alone would be worth the drive up here. I hear many different foreign languages being spoken. Off we go to explore.

We find the Whitney trailhead bulletin board. *Red Dog. Thursday. Camp. Fire Weed.* Cryptic notes translatable only to those in the know. Mac notes a flyer: *Hot Showers: Kirk's Barber Shop, Lone Pine.* We find the Mount Whitney trailhead and up we go. I love the beginning of a trail. I know that I probably won't be the same when I return.

> *The old trail (from the west end of the portal) started off steep and narrow and was considered to be the worst part of the trip. But all that has changed. The new trail ascends gradually across a chaparral slope dominated by sagebrush, pinyon pine and manzanita. Instead of being the worst, this is now about the easiest section of the entire trip. Easiest, that is, except for the heat, which can be most aggravating on a hot summer day. An early departure from the trailhead is thus well advised.*

> — Paul Hellweg and Scott McDonald,
> *Mount Whitney Guide for Hikers and Climbers*

We start up at about 11:30 a.m. Piece of cake. Up, up, up. Folks hike down the trail and folks hike up. We don't plan to climb the entire eleven miles to the summit; we're just going to check out the trail. This is a scouting mission. The trail is well marked and well used. After about half-a-mile we cross a little creek. We step across rocks with a downhill drop on our left. I can't imagine this stream in the springtime when the snowmelt is heavy.

My foot feels normal. It feels better today than it did yesterday. I'm so thankful that I am able to be on a trail again. The walk is easy and picturesque. Every now and then I pause to view the Owens Valley below us to the east.

We stop for lunch at Lone Pine Lake, elevation 9,960 feet. The deep blue of the water mirrors the deep blue of the sky. Foxtail pine trees surround the lake. Other people explore the lake too. A man on a boulder to the north of us appears to be taking a nap. A lady walking on the beach to the south picks up litter. A group of male and female teenagers, or early twenties, come down the trail then take off to the far end of the lake. This is a great spot for lunch so we find a rock and relax with a picnic break.

Up, up, up. Back on the trail.

> *MILE 3.5: Atop the small crest, a sign announces that you're entering Bighorn Park, which is a willow-covered meadow that was once a shallow lake. From the crest, the trail drops slightly and skirts the meadow on its south side.*
> — *Mount Whitney Guide for Hikers and Climbers*

At the far end of Bighorn Park is Outpost Camp, elevation 10,365 feet. The camp is virtually empty, not one tent. The map shows another camp further up, Trail Camp, elevation 12,039 feet, at MILE 6.3. Maybe everyone is up there. The trail is full of mostly day hikers. We read that this is a slow time but I can't imagine "busy" if this is not.

A waterfall animates the far end of the camping area. I walk over to the solar latrine that looks way out-of-place sitting here in the middle of this pristine wilderness. The hardware must have been delivered by helicopter.

[NOTE: The Forest Service has since removed the solar latrines from Outpost Camp and Trail Camp.]

We move on, passing through a lupine wildflower meadow, where the lupines are as tall as me. I feel like Alice in Wonderland walking through a maze of giant flowers. I'd love to come back here in the spring. Mac and I plan to apply for a permit to climb Mount Whitney, that must be postmarked March 1 to May 31 next year. The quota system had to be created because of the number of people wishing to hike to the summit of Whitney. The quota season is from May 22 to October 15. Before and after those dates campers still need wilderness permits but there's no quota.

"I have an idea!" I claim.

Mac rolls his eyes.

I continue, "Why don't we get married up on Whitney summit? Who could we get to perform the ceremony? Who else could make it to the top? Your mom wouldn't like the idea. Thom would make it. Jeremiah. Mike Martin. Steve and Laura. Aja probably wouldn't want to go, unless Heather went too. Sunshine might, . . ." I'm talking to myself by now. Maybe the high elevation and thin air have made me wacky.

Soon we meet plenty of switchbacks up to Mirror Lake. The lake area has been overused in the past, so it is now closed to camping, hoping for a revival of the vegetation. A group of Boy Scouts is down by the shore checking it out. The beauty here is indescribable. I just don't have words other than magnificent, spectacular, incredible, divine, glorious and unbelievable. I would like to be an artist with words, like Colin Fletcher, to give this scenery a proper poetic description.

The trail levels off slightly and we may be above tree line because I don't see any. Above us, rocks. Below us sparkles Mirror Lake. The trail continues up but we decide we'd better start back down. It's 3:30 p.m. and we would like to hike down while there's still daylight. It's a good thing Mac is practical, because I'd hike up another half-a-mile just to see Consultation Lake. It's another six miles to the summit. Everyone seems to be going down the trail now. We sit for a bit and check out the peaks through the binoculars. The mountaineering route up Whitney is different from this trail. The mountaineering route goes straight up through the rocks.

We join the flow of traffic going downhill. It's easier on the heart and lungs going down but harder on the knees. We catch up to a limping hiker and stop to talk. His left knee is wrapped and braced. "It's much easier for me to go up. I climbed Whitney today in 5½ hours but it's taking me longer to come down."

Hm-m. That's two miles an hour. We walk on. *If he can climb to the summit, then so can I.* This feeds my imagination and lets my mind wander.

A couple miles later I notice a man hiking up the trail toward us. His *energy* catches my attention. His body looks strong and he carries a huge pack. He wears a gigantic smile with lily-white teeth. I want to talk with him but feel intimidated by his enormous *energy*. It is good *energy* but it is so massive. I shy away, hoping he'll speak first. As he passes by us I turn around to watch him walk away. Strapped to his backpack are snowshoes. The smile makes sense now. It looks like he plans to be *out there* for a while. I want to be him.

The hike down is just as beautiful as the hike up, except we don't have to turn around to see the Owens Valley; it is right in our view. I imagine being up here with snowshoes in the springtime and expect that most of these streams would be a challenge to cross.

It's still light as we near the trailhead. Mac gets *barn sour* again and takes off for the car.

We unload our daypacks then walk over to the little gift shop/store/café. We buy postcards, some topo maps, and an aerial photographed map of Mount Whitney taken from different directions.

As we drive away, Mac stops by the bulletin board and asks me to jot down the phone numbers for the hot showers at the barbershop.

We drive down the road and stop by the Lone Pine Campground to pick up clean clothes and toiletries. In town, we locate the barbershop, Kirk's. There's a sign that says the key can be picked up at Gardiner's Sporting Goods Store. Down the block, Gardiner's sign says, *OPEN* but it's locked. The lights and the cash register are on.

Mac calls the *after hours* phone number and gets an answering machine. He leaves the message that we'll wait out in front of the barbershop for about fifteen minutes. I sit. Mac goes across the street to buy groceries. The *Sierra Nevada Natural History* book keeps me company. Groups of people pass by, most of them speaking foreign languages. Tourists. I keep my eyes open for the possible barbershop connection.

Mac returns. We give up on the hot showers and decide to go back to camp. As we U-turn and pass Gardiner's again, someone appears in the window and the store looks open now. Mac runs in and makes arrangements. We drive to find the alley and the building. The door is unlocked. We go in and check for other people. Empty. It's kind of dumpy and dark, counting three showers and one private bathroom. Funky but, hopefully, functional. An inside open door leads into the barbershop with a pool table. I close the doors, thinking someone forgot, and I get into the shower. Oh joy, rapture. A hot shower when you haven't had one in days and have been climbing on the Mount Whitney trail feels divine. Ah-h-h-h. I stay longer than necessary.

I hear Mac shuffling around and expressing joyful sounds. I hear him finish before me and leave the shower area.

When I finish I go into the barbershop where I find a sign on the pool table that reads:

Welcome to Kirk's Barber Shop. If the showers are full, please relax, play some pool, and have fun. We invite you to sign the guest register. Thank you.
— Kirk

Mac has signed the register. Oh, how small town is this? I remember small town kindness and have missed it.

Back at camp we cook *fajitas*. Does it get better than this?

Sitting around the fire after dinner, we are quiet. I can't think of anything to say. I'm tired, full and happy. Mac sits and puffs on his cigar.

My neck gets tired from sitting and looking up at the stars. I ask, "You wanna spread out the tarp and lie here under the stars? If we had lounge chairs we could just lay out here in our sleeping bags." I wait for a *yes*.

He doesn't go for it. I spread out on the picnic table and watch the night sky.

Soon we turn in. We have to go home tomorrow. I ask the Universe to wake me up early again for the sunrise.

September 24, Sunday ☉ ♍
Day Four, The Scenic Route

I pop up, unzip the tent and see that the timing is again perfect. It's still dark with a faint light to the east. *Thank you, Universe.* Again, I dress in warm clothes, grab the camera and take off for higher ground. As always, other folks are up walking around. I head up the trail toward Whitney and decide to walk further up the trail this morning than yesterday.

Coming back I see Mac up and at 'em at campsite #22, so I scurry "home." I've been gone a long time.

After a leisurely breakfast, we hit the road. We drive north on Highway 395, marveling at the magnificent peaks to our west. We stop at Manzanar War Relocation Center, a National Historic Site, the Japanese-American internment camp during World War II. Years ago Mac and I met Jeanne Wakatsuki Houston and James D. Houston, authors of *Farewell to Manzanar*. I haven't read it yet.

We drive further north on Highway 395, turn west on an unmarked road and drive to the Manzanar white obelisk at the old cemetery. In the tumbleweed next to the graves are sprinkled brightly-colored paper origami birds. I find a baby's grave, probably born and died here in the prison. I become overwhelmed by the *energy* and begin to cry. Then I feel a great pain deep within my being, grab my heart and begin to weep. Mac walks over and holds me. He's feeling it too. We stand together for a long time, holding each other.

I'll bet it's unbearably hot here in the summer. The high desert is spectacular with Mount Williamson in the distance. It's beautiful but how could the United States government have done that to American citizens? They did it to the Native Americans too. How dare they.

As we continue the drive north my thoughts are still at Manzanar. The valley is hot and beautiful. I look at the map. We had intended to stop at Onion Valley but somehow we've missed it. I plan to read *Farewell to Manzanar* when we get home.

The incredible scenery continues. Mac wants to check out Convict Lake, just past Crowley Lake. We take the short drive off 395 and the lake is peppered with fishermen and fisherwomen. The lake is a mile across. We stop at a little bridge that crosses the spillway. A lovely lady dressed in a long, flowing skirt, sits on the rocks watching the trout. If I were an artist I would paint this scene. At least a dozen good-sized trout plant themselves at the spillway, facing the lake and the rushing water. Fisherpersons try to snag these beauties but the fish are not biting. The biggest of all trout is located right where the flow begins to topple. I can almost reach down and grab her/him.

Back on the road and a few miles north, Mac takes Highway 203 into the Mammoth Region where he had gone camping with John and Scott last month. He wants to show it to me. We leave the desert and drive up into the lush and fragrant pine forests.

Mammoth is home to big, shiny ski resorts. Off-season, mountain bikers use the lifts and the runs. We go up and head toward the valley. The view from up here is breathtaking. This would be a great place to start *The Sierra Garden Tour*. The Pacific Crest Trail (PCT) and the John Muir Trail (JMT) go right through the valley passing Rainbow Falls, Devil's Postpile and Minaret Falls. The John Muir Wilderness is to the south. The Ansel Adams Wilderness is to the west and the north.

We descend and Mac points out Agnew Meadows where he wanted to camp but John and Scott out-voted him. We drive through the valley, park and walk up to Devil's Postpile National Monument. This is off-season and again, I can't imagine this during the busy season. The crowd of people swarms and flows. It's a very easy walk. I feel kind of silly in my hiking clothes, hat and daypack. The walk could be done in high heels. But it is beautiful. The Postpile is a natural phenomenon. I expected it to be sitting out in the wilderness. The pictures I've seen of it haven't included the visitor viewing platforms and the fences. We don't have time to go up on top, where the hexagonal shapes are laid out like a tile patio; we have a long drive ahead of us today. We don't have time for the 1½-mile walk to the falls. We'll just have to come back. I could easily spend an entire season right here.

Back on Highway 395 we pass Mono Lake and turn west on Highway 120 toward Tioga Pass. Mac has never been in Yosemite Valley. We hope to arrive with plenty of daylight left to see the sights.

The views from Tioga Pass and Tuolumne Meadows are awesome! The PCT and JMT go right through Tuolumne Meadows, where there's a visitor center and a store. We walk into the store and the place is packed with French tourists speaking loudly and buying weird little trinkets. The store is a combination gift shop, grocery and camping equipment outfitting department store. It has everything from fresh produce, silly Yosemite souvenirs, to sleeping bags and tents. I go next door and buy some French fries.

We drive on and stop at Olmsted Point, an outlook with a view of Half Dome. Across the canyon we see Clouds Rest, a spot up a trail from Yosemite Valley. It's majestic and cold up here.

We have enough daylight to cruise Yosemite Valley. I drive so Mac can look. It's been many, many years since I've been here. The waterfalls are late-season trickles but they're still magnificent. We drive all the way to the end and start to loop back. Once again, this is off-season. The traffic is moderate and the campgrounds are full. We drive past the "hiker's only" campground and see hundreds of tents packed closely together. "That's obscene," I say and take a photo of the colored tent mass. Ah, the wilderness.

Down the road I see cars parked and folks standing on the side of the road with binoculars looking up. El Capitan. I stop. Mac gets out and looks up. Soon he spots a climber. Then another. He gets the binoculars. He sees more and more climbers. We count at least fifteen people up there hanging by who-knows-what on that huge rock face. From down here it looks like the rock face slants outward and that they'd fall right off. We watch for some time then drive on our way. We have to go home. The sun sets as we wind downhill with the Merced River.

September 25, Monday ☽ ♎
Day Five, Home

To my surprise I wake up at dawn's early light. I get up and go for a walk to watch the sunrise. I find a perfect spot a couple of blocks away by Aja's bus stop where I can see the color waking up on the wharf, the city and Monterey Bay. I love traveling and also I love being home.

September 28, Thursday ☽ ♏
Dawn's Early Light

I've never been a morning person but since the Whitney trip I've been getting up every morning at dawn's early light to watch the sunrise. It's becoming an unusual hobby of mine now and I love it! The sunrise is a gift that is ours for the taking and I've become quite fond of the routine. It makes the rest of the day so special.

Thank you Mount Whitney.

October 11, Wednesday ☽ ♉
Miah's Birthday

I'd like to say a word about my son, Jeremiah Scott-Thomas Pendleton. He's twenty years old today and has lived in Rico, Colorado since January. Jeremiah is a gift and I thank the Universe for sending him to me. He got me back on the right track, spiritually.

He was such a beautiful little child. His hair was a curly, golden blond. The light shined in his smile. He's a brilliant being.

When he was young, just barely old enough to talk but not that old, he came to me one morning. I was in the kitchen and he had just awakened. He was quite excited and rubbing the sleep from his eyes. With great enthusiasm and joy he said, "Muthoo, Muthoo. I saw her. I saw my wife. She's so beautiful," with his face beaming bright. "I love her so much!" Then suddenly, a sadness took over his being, his light dimmed, . . . then he spoke, "I miss her so much." He was young, not more than three. I was speechless. The look on his face was wise and sincere. I believe that in his sleep he had slipped over to *The Other Side* and mingled with the spirits, his Beloved.

With that moment he reminded me of my spiritual Self that I had pushed aside many years earlier when I was a child.

Thank you for being Jeremiah. Thank you for being my son. You are so lovable and I miss having you near. I love you.

I go through some papers and coincidentally find this journal entry that I wrote last January:

January 6, ☼ ♑ / ☽ ♓

My 19-year-old son, Jeremiah, just left to go work at a resort in Telluride, Colorado. The job is for four months and more if he chooses. This morning as he finishes packing, I remember that I was nineteen when I left home too. I decide to tell him the story. "I remember the day I moved out. It was January 6th!" *Déjà vu.* As the words unfold I say, "Your dad moved in about a month later, in February."

It's important that we acknowledge and celebrate coincidences. It's the Universe's way of getting our attention and letting us know that a Higher Power exists to love and help guide us.

My son may be a high-powered and rowdy hormone-charged 19-year-old, but I'm so proud of

143

him and in awe of his spiritual sensitivity. He's always been my teacher and friend. God gives us our children for such a short time. So love them dearly.

I love you Jeremiah Scott-Thomas Pendleton. May your light shine on others as you have shined on me. Peace. Love. Joy. Abundance and good health. Thank you for choosing me. I'm so proud to be your mother.

November 11, Saturday ☼ ♏ / ☾ ♋

Merrily, merrily, merrily, merrily. Life is but a dream.

When I dream, *that* dream seems to be the current reality. It remains reality until I wake up. *This* reality, sitting with pen in hand, is also a dream. When we die (or leave our Earthly bodies) we wake up from this dream. The beauty of this waking reality is that as humans we've been given the gift of free will and choice. What we usually lack in this reality is awareness. When we become more aware we realize that this is a dream and we can choose to do whatever we wish in this reality.

Two books come to mind, *The Right Use of Will* (a channeled piece) and *The Seat of the Soul* by Gary Zukav. I read the first book years ago and it led me down a trail of self examination and realization. The second book *The Seat of the Soul* came to me during a very troubled time of my life and answered many of my questions.

One concept that I extracted from Zukav, (and this is my interpretation) has to do with these realities: First, you have to believe that time is non-linear. Time is a human-made concept. With no beginning and no end, we can come and go in time at will. (It's a difficult concept for some to believe, but I have learned that belief systems can be changed. I call *belief systems, . . .* B.S.) Then, when the concept of reincarnation surfaces, Zukav allowed me to believe that instead of *past* lives, we can be living *simultaneous* lives. The act of sleeping frees the soul. For example, in this reality I can be Ellen, sitting here in the chair writing. When I slip into that dream state, the energy that I call my soul can occupy another reality, perhaps that of a monk in Tibet. Then as the soul slips into another state of reality it could take on another life, perhaps that of a baker in Paris.

What we learn in this reality on a consciousness level becomes a part of the soul and travels with the soul energy. It's the only thing we can take with us from this life on Earth. So what I learn here on Earth in the way of life lessons can be taken back or forward in time to my other realities or lives.

Emotions are tools that can guide us to areas of our being that might want attention. Emotion, [< L. *e-*, out + *movere*, to move]. Listen to our emotions. Pay attention. Learn to step outside of our selves and observe. Become a witness. Get into touch with our Higher Self, our inner voice, our guru within. Become intimate with it. Learn to trust it and let it become the decision maker in our lives.

Another concept I extracted from *The Seat of the Soul* is that our mind, ego, personality and body are tools created by our spirit energy to be used for the evolution of our consciousness. We are, in essence, spiritual in nature, cosmic spirits in human form. Oftentimes we forget this. We let our ego rule our Earth reality. We let our personality rule. We let our body rule. We let our mind rule. We forget why we're here and get distracted. When we remember our true Self, we begin to address the lessons that are offered to us here on Earth and hopefully take action to learn and master them.

To *Love thy Self* is an activity, spending quality time with the Self. Meditation eliminates the mind (thoughts), the body (physical sensations), the ego (results) and the personality (Earth reality). Yet these are all tools created by the spirit to be used. In the state of meditation we are pure spirit, the Universal energy. And like any other area in our lives, the more time, attention or love we give to an area, the more it can develop and evolve. We become intimate with our Self. Love thyself. It is not selfish; it is Self first. The more intimate we become with our Self, the more intimate we become with the Universe. Intimate [< L. *intus*, within].

Well, I've been on my high horse this morning. Time to climb off.

November 12, Sunday ○ ♋
Au Naturale

I read in the letter section of *Backpacker* magazine that lime juice works as a mosquito repellent. *Just squeeze a little juice into your hand and spread.* I almost hate to say this, but I can't wait to try it.

December 8, Friday ☼♐/○ ♋

The fool who persists in his folly will become wise.
— William Blake

Mac got a new book, *Adventure Trekking, A Handbook for Independent Travelers* by Robert Strauss. It covers the globe. Looks good.

I checked out two books from the library that look interesting: *My Tibet* by photographer Galen Rowell and the Dalai Lama, and *Freedom in Exile, The Autobiography of the Dalai Lama.* What is it about Tibet that intrigues me? Have I been there before?

PART VIII — *Mount Whitney*

January 1, Monday ☼ ♑ / ◯ ♉
Happy New Year!

No man ever followed his genius till it misled him.
　　　　　　 — Henry David Thoreau, *Walden*

genius, [< L., guardian spirit] — *Webster's New World Dictionary*

New Year's Eve is no biggie at our house; New Year's Day is the big eating fest and celebration. Mac's mom, Deko, is from Japan and traditionally, New Year's Day is a big holiday of the year. Deko and I cooked and cleaned all day yesterday. Japanese food is served all day January 1. It's an open house that goes from noon until everyone goes home, passes out or falls asleep. We start the day with a ritual *sake* ceremonial toast to one's good health, happiness and prosperity; one small cup for each blessing. Everyone who enters the house drinks *sake* from the three tiny cups, makes three wishes and gets a New Year's blessing and hug from me. Repeat attendees look forward to the party every year.

This year I invited Colin but he hasn't showed up yet. He's currently in a self-imposed isolation, *purdah,* as he calls it. He's birthing his next book, *River.* When he was 70 years old, he backpacked to the headwaters of the Colorado River. Then he hiked, following the water until the river got big enough to boat. Solo, he paddled the Colorado River down to the Gulf of Mexico. As the day turns to night I give up on him. He probably gets a lot of invites.

When the light turns dark, I build a fire in the backyard fire pit, then invite the folks in the house to sit by the fire in the moonlight, if they'd like. As I walk up the driveway to retrieve another chair from the front porch, Colin pulls up and parks his car. How pleasant. He apologizes and explains that he had been hitting tennis balls with his ball machine all afternoon and was running on *Fletcher time.* He brings a lovely bottle of Cabernet Sauvignon with a personalized label saying, *Greetings, Colin Fletcher.* He is very hungry and goes straight for food.

Chicago Steve gathers Mac, Colin and me together, fills a Norse horn with Champagne and initiates a New Year toast. We take turns as everyone follows Steve's lead, stating our New Year resolution and drinking from the horn. Mac resolves to lose weight, spend more time out-of-doors and hike to the summit of Mount Whitney.

I gather myself, take a deep breath and speak what comes as it comes through me: "Let me acknowledge, identify, understand, accept and overcome all of my fears and turn them into love." When I hear and realize what

I've just said, I gasp. I'm surprised since I've never thought these words before.

Colin takes the next turn, "My resolution this year is the same as it was last year and the year before that and the year before that: Not to make any New Year resolutions."

"Here, here," we chime in unison.

The evening evolves. At one point I stand outside with Colin on the back porch and talk about campfires. He says, "I feel the campfire scares away all the little animals who would otherwise come to visit. And, . . ." he stops himself midway, "Oh, I write about it in one of my books."

I understand. I rely upon my writings to explain my thoughts. I feel that I write better than I can speak. The problem with me is that I change my mind. What I thought last year, may not be the same today. I'm not that consistent but more fluid and mutable. *We change our minds because we can.* But maybe that's not really a problem. I feel lucky to know Colin. I love listening to him, his stories and his fading Welsh accent. He says it takes him five years to complete a book. I feel honored and humbled by his presence.

January 3, Wednesday ◯ v/c (void of course)
Loose Ends

Curiosity killed the cat. But for a while, . . . I was suspect.
— Steven Wright

I just called the Mount Whitney ranger station. Mac and I would like to hike to the summit this year. I wrote a letter last September inquiring about how to apply for a wilderness permit and they said that the reservation system will be changing this year and to call back in January. That's now. The recording said that the *office will be closed until a federal budget is passed or a continuing resolution is signed.* Government. Politics.

February 21, Wednesday ☿♓ /☉♈
Sweet

Jeremiah has returned from Colorado. He and a friend drove all the way with the truck full of Miah's belongings. His friend couldn't stay; he had to drive on. Miah looks great. It's nice to have him back. It's been hard worrying about him from so far away. Now I can worry about him close by.

March 20, Wednesday ☿ ♈ /☉♈
Whitney I

Coincidence is God's way of remaining anonymous.
— Albert Einstein

The Mount Whitney wilderness permit application arrived today along with the Yosemite High Country map that I ordered from Tom Harrison Cartography. Lovely map; the contours come alive. I like the way the Harrison maps are shaded. Now we have to decide first and second choices, alternate dates for the Whitney trip.

April 1, Monday ☉♍
Whitney II

We mail our Mount Whitney wilderness reservation applications. July 11, is my first priority, with July 18, September 26, September 5 as the alternative dates. They're all Thursdays with Sundays as our exit day. Mac fills one out too with September 26 being his first choice. I drop them off at the post office at about 7:20 a.m. before Sunshine and I drive to San Jose airport. She's going to visit a friend in Palm Springs.

Gift today: A big, yellow spider on my poppy plant. A vibrant, completely lemon yellow spider. The body looks like a Black Widow. It moves like a pollen-covered bee backing out of the purple poppy.

April 7, Sunday ☽ ♐
Easter

Leave it as it is. You cannot improve upon it; not a bit. The ages have been at work on it, and man can only mar it.

— President Theodore Roosevelt

"What do you want to do today?" Mac asks.

Without hesitation or doubt I reply, "Go for a hike." And we do. Daylight Savings Time started today. We both have things to do before we leave so we don't get going until about 12:30 p.m. We decide on Garland Ranch Regional Park in Carmel Valley. Mac wants to hike up to Snively's Ridge. We park. In celebration of Easter, I wear my wide-brimmed black straw hat with black and white silk flowers. Hiking boots, walking shorts, backpack and an Easter hat. But when I step out of the car, the wind whips through and it might be a problem keeping my hat on. I tuck my long braid inside the hat and the added girth makes a tight fit. We cross the Carmel River. I hold onto my hat going over the bridge, just in case it tries to fly away.

"Did you bring the map or do we need to go get one?" Mac asks.

I didn't bring it so we walk the 200 yards over to the visitor's center. On the new map it looks as though the park boundaries have been extended since our last map. New trails stretch out on both sides of the original park boundary. We take off on the Lupine Loop Trail that circles a flood plain. As the trail climbs up into the trees the wind stops. Baby spring flowers welcome us.

"I forgot it! I forgot my flower book. Haven't I learned that lesson yet?"

"Field guides. They're called *field* guides because they're made to bring out into the *field*," Mac gently teases. "I'm surprised you didn't even bring the laminated cards." (*Mac's Field Guide to Northern California Wildflowers* and *Mac's Field Guide to Southern California Wildflowers*, 7"x 11" double-sided plastic laminated cards with about forty or so wildflower pictures on each side. Lightweight and handy to carry for identification purposes.)

"Darn. I can't believe I forgot them."

We walk up Mesa Trail to Fern Trail. Up, up, up. "Okay, now what's this?" picking some miner's lettuce and holding it up for a quiz. I eat it. Mac doesn't guess so I tell him. "What's this?" pointing to maidenhair fern. Again unsuccessful guesses and I tell him. "I know it has medicinal properties but I don't know what they are." I make a note to look it up when I get home. (I did remember to bring my notepad and pencil.) Occasionally we pass a California bay laurel tree. The smells are heavenly. I snatch a bay leaf, crush it, and lift it to my nose. It feels so good to be back out here. Snively's Ridge is 2.5 miles uphill from the visitor's center. All uphill. The climb heats us up quickly. We're mostly in the shade but the air is warm.

Up, up, up. We stop at the junction of Fern and Sky Trails where a claw foot bathtub catches the spring water and holds a tub full for horses and dogs to drink. I wet my hands. Mac dips his ball cap in, fills it, and pours it over his head. I like being hot, but Mac loves being cool. (He's cool, he's cool.)

We hear folks coming up the trail so we take off up Sky Trail. As we go up, fewer and fewer trees grow providing less and less shade. It gets pretty hot. The view of Carmel Valley becomes spectacular. The Santa Cruz Mountains, Fremont Peak and Mount Toro line the horizon. I love it up here. That's the hawk in me.

"We're almost there," Mac guides.

The trail opens out onto a lovely flat spot overlooking a range to the south. I plop myself down in the grass and guzzle some water. The fire tower looks over us from the west. A trail to another hilltop beckons. I sit and sniff the warm spring air. No bugs. A jogger clad in shoes, socks, red shorts, wristwatch and a headband runs up from whence we came, stops at the trail marker, clicks his wristwatch, puffs and huffs. The fog spreads out below on the Monterey Bay. Mac offers the man (presumably older than us) water. He says he had plenty before he started but then accepts. He looks in great shape. I can't believe he just ran up what we had such a difficult time walking.

"How long did it take you?" I ask.

"Thirty-three minutes. That's good. Last time it took me forty-three minutes."

It took us an hour and a half. I am impressed.

Two hikers walk up the trail. The top of the world is crowded today, . . . but it is a holiday. They plop down on the bench. The woman recognizes the trail runner, "Didn't you write that article in the newspaper about hiking with your daughter?"

"Yes. That was the Bryce Canyon trip."

"Didn't you have to bribe her to get her to go?"

My ears perk up, "Bribe? How did you bribe her?"

"Jelly beans."

"How old is she?" I figure she'd have to be pretty young to fall for the old jelly bean trick.

"Eleven when we started but now she's thirteen."

We talk about kids, hiking and camping. Mac recognizes the man and asks if it is him. Yes, it is. He wrote a couple of articles freelance for the newspaper where Mac works and states an interest in having the paper publish more internationally-oriented travel articles. "Everyone on the Monterey Peninsula travels the globe," the jogger/writer states.

Everyone but me.

The three of them talk more of local issues while I study the map. The other couple takes off down the trail we had planned to travel. As we prepare to follow I point to what might be the new addition to the park, the Redwood Canyon, and ask if that is so. Yes, and he guides us, giving map directions and trail tips. He offers some information about other new trails further on and alternate parking spots to those trails. *Thanks,* and we're off.

Beyond the horse corral, Snively's Ridge drops off quickly. *Very steep,* the map warns. Yes, we slip and slide downhill. Soon we catch up to the other couple. "Do you want to see a Horned Toad?" they ask.

I grin, turn red and confess, "I've always called them *Horny Toads.*"

They point into the bushes and sitting there, camouflaged by its own coloring, I finally spot it. *Cool.* The couple takes off down the trail.

"You're a horny toad," Mac teases. "I live with a frog and a horny toad." (Jeremiah's nickname is *Frog* or *Froggie.*) Mac amuses himself and continues to tease me.

Down, down, down. The trail drops off. We come to the crossroads and, surprisingly, Mac takes the Garzas Creek trail heading toward the Redwood Canyon. The other couple takes the trail back toward the visitor's center. *Whoopee!! I love new trails.* The jogger/writer had warned us that it might not turn out to be quicker if we take "shortcuts." He advised us to stay on the trail. We listen, even though I am tempted to cut across certain spots. Garzas Creek speaks loudly as we descend into the canyon. When we reach the creek, we are greeted by chilly air, a newly constructed bridge and a lovely (but I'm sure, cold) swimming hole. Mac dips his hat into the stream and showers himself with the cool water. I stop on the bridge and check the map. Soon the East Ridge and Redwood Canyon Trails would fork. We pause briefly then walk on to find it.

The creek crossing consists of a couple of shaky 2"x 12" boards. The creek trail seems new and obviously not used very much. The next creek crossing has to be done across rocks. I find a stick to use as a third leg. The creek is small but big enough to get us plenty wet if we fall in. I tuck the binoculars into my pack just in case I slip. Mac goes first. I start to cross. The last rock looks like a stretch for my legs. In the middle, I switch feet so I can get a strong push off. Mac grabs my hand and helps me. Without it, I might not have made it across gracefully, if at all.

After a few more board crossings and following the creek a bit, the trail climbs uphill. Ah, the Redwood Canyon. Redwood trees, *Sequoia sempervirens*. The tallest one is in Northern California and is almost 380 feet tall, five stories higher than the Statue of Liberty. Their horizontal roots spread out and weave with other nearby redwood roots creating a strong network, holding each other up. The redwood grove fragrance fills my being with joy. Lots of newly fallen trees and branches scatter across the forest floor. This reminds me of the redwood canyon up Soberanes Creek and how defined and worn it is compared to this trail. This is a baby new trail.

We hike up, up, up. The creek disappears. I suppose it has either dried up or begins running underground. I stop to touch a giant tree. How fast we must seem to move to them. We probably speed by like tiny, flying insects with the wind to our backs.

Back on the trail I start to get tired. *Perhaps it's time to turn back?* I hear something. It's either running water or the blood gushing through my brain. *Water.* The creek rejoins us. I look at the map. The trail dead ends half a mile up. We could retrace our steps or cross the creek and travel the Terrace Trail. Mac cools himself off at the creek.

"We should have brought the water filter. How much water do you have left?" Mac asks.

"I have plenty. Help yourself."

"Would you like a half of a bagel?" Mac offers part of a poppy seed bagel.

We choose the Terrace Trail and ascend out of the cool canyon back into the hot, spring hillside. *How easy it is to climb out of the shade,* looking back down on the treetops. The trail becomes very narrow. I should be keeping my eyes on the trail but a hawk soars close by and I get out the binoculars for a better look. A red-tailed hawk. The best part about being a hawk must be catching those updrafts and sailing free in the wind.

The trail levels out and I hear what could be a deer running alongside the hill. I stop, look, then give a body hug to a huge, blue bush lupine. The wildflowers on the hillside demand immediate attention. Blankets of little yellow blossoms, blue ones, purple, vibrant red Indian Paintbrush, ... Oh, the beauty.

While I'm busy looking at the flowers Mac walks on down the trail out of sight. The trail descends and switches back five or six times, with Mac down below and me up above. I run to catch up. When I do, Mac warns against running on this trail. "You don't want to trip and fall down there, do you?" as he points down the hillside.

Suddenly, I realize how high up we are and how steep the hill is. "It's a good thing we're not acrophobic, eh?"

"If I fell, I'd beat you down the hill," Mac refers to our weight difference.

No fear. I feel quite at home out here on this narrow trail, . . . a memory, perhaps, from my deer days.

Soon I sense we are going in a direction away from the visitors center and stop to look at the map. "Uh, oh."

"What?"

"We might have a problem." We look at the map but Mac doesn't seem too disturbed. The Terrace Trail doesn't go back to the visitors center but ends on East Garzas Road next to the Carmel River.

"We can walk down the road back to the park," Mac observes. "East Garzas, then a left on Via Las Encinas, right on Paso Del Rio. An easement trail begins there. Yeah. Okay," and off we go. We pass a sign facing the opposite direction welcoming hikers to Garland Ranch. We're on the right trail. We come upon a small trail going in the direction back to the visitors center. I sense it might be a shortcut toward meeting our destination.

"Do you know where it goes for sure?" Mac asks.

"No. Not for sure," I wish I did. I'm willing to venture out, but Mac is right; getting lost could add hours to our journey and it is almost five o'clock. We meet the road and a sign marking the easement trail to Garland Ranch through private property donated by the Condon family.

It feels strange to walk down the road with asphalt, houses, cars and trucks. We walk down East Garzas Road past the bridge to Carmel Valley Road at Boronda Road, many blocks, but a pleasant walk. Friendly horses corralled along the way come to greet us, probably out of boredom. We turn left on Via Las Encinas then right on Paso Del Rio, our road to river easement. Finally at the end of Paso Del Rio, we find the signs welcoming us back to Garland Ranch. Ah-h, back on a dirt road. The Carmel Valley River roars close by. Down the road and then, . . . the river. No bridge. The river. We look upstream and downstream. We look on the map. No bridge. The flow is too swift and too deep for us to cross without ropes. On the map we find another easement trail further up Via Las Encinas and start walking. The trail is in the shadow of a hillside and the air begins to get chilly. We put on our extra clothes. Up, up, up.

We find the park easement and join Mesa Trail. My knees start to feel worn. It is so beautiful, however, and I feel glad to be here. Mac becomes barn sour and trots off ahead of me. We head downhill on Vaquero trail, one I remember traveling the other direction on a walk with my friend Genie. The trail is narrow, for hikers only. No mountain bikes, no horses. I remember a waterfall close by. Genie and I saw a huge Great Horned Owl sitting on a rock ledge above the waterfall. I keep my eyes open. As I round the curve a hawk screeches and I see Mac's teal-colored shirt exit the waterfall area. I return the screech. The acoustics in this rocky bowl area make it fun to talk and listen to the hawk. It screeches again and we continue back and forth for a while. I slow down because of the descending steps of the narrow pathway and because my eyes search for the nearby hawk who I can hear, but not see. I would like to stay much longer talking with the hawks, but I have to catch up to Mac. We are still up, up, up on the hillside and have a way to go.

I hear the river rumbling on the right and soon it appears. We drop down and level out onto the flood plain and rejoin the Lupine Loop. We've probably walked seven to ten miles. I'll be sore tomorrow. The breeze picks up in the flatland. Heading into the wind my Easter hat flips off more than once.

Thinking about what to cook for dinner tonight and guessing something has been on his mind to have kept him going at such a fast pace to the end, I ask Mac, "While you were walking today, did you think about any special food you might want for dinner tonight?"

After only a slight hesitation he answers, "Margaritas."

April 13, Saturday ☽♓
Wilderness Permits

I can't wait to go to my post office box and see if my Whitney wilderness permit has arrived. Mac received his yesterday. The date they gave him is July 18, my second choice.

Yes!! I got one. My date of entry is September 26, Mac's first choice. Hm-m. Oh well, we've got two four-day overnight wilderness permits to climb Mount Whitney. I'm so excited.

Mac had the sniffles last night and today it crested into a full blown cold. We stay in and watch movies. I would recommend all three of these: *Home for the Holidays, The Prophecy,* and *Strange Days.*

June 24, Monday ☼♋/☽♎
Countdown

Twenty-three days until we leave for our Mount Whitney trip. I weighed in this morning at 111 pounds. I don't have any weight to lose but need to get strong and exercise my lungs. The countdown has begun. My backpack needs a minor repair. After I do that, I can fill it with weight and take it for some more practice walks. Oh, I wait impatiently to be in the Sierra. My heart fills with joy just thinking about it. Perhaps I should abandon my pen and take a practice hike instead of write. Namaste.

July 2, Tuesday ○≋

Angels fly because they take themselves lightly.
— G.K. Chesterton

Fifteen days and counting until Mount Whitney. Yesterday I rode my bicycle from Monterey, over the hill to Rio Road in Carmel and back. The weather was hot until I got to the top of Carmel hill. Then the fog-cooled breeze dropped the temperature at least ten degrees. Good workout.

I'm packing my backpack, preparing to take it for a "practice pack." I put together a Car Camping Checklist; maybe I'll put one together for backpacking. I don't want to forget anything.

I load up my pack with water, clothes, cooking gear, books, canned food, . . . anything to add weight. Thirty-five pounds and a couple miles. I hoist up my pack, settle it on my back and hips, adjust the straps and leave home.

Up Jefferson Street. It feels good. At the top of Jefferson I turn on High Street then left on Harrison. A city work truck drives by, stops, backs up and the driver says, "Are you looking for Veterans Park?"

"No," I answer. "But thank you."

They look confused and drive on. Veterans Park is at the top of Jefferson and the only camping spot in Monterey.

I catch up with them again at the top of Harrison, where they're working at a manhole. I understand their confusion yet I don't explain. I would if they ask.

I continue walking up through the Defense Language Institute, turning around occasionally to take in the view of Monterey Bay and Mount Toro. I cross

Prescott, one of the steepest hills in Monterey. The walk home feels good with the muscles beginning to come alive.

July 7, Sunday ☽♈
Lighten Up

Drum up the quest for a lasting peace and unconditional love in our times. Let your voice rise like a fountain in prayer for a lasting watertight peace. Let your hands pound out healing rhythms on your drums. Celebrate life! Evoke the spirit of the ancestors. Give thanks to our Creator (Obatala)! Let peace begin with you! Let love reign supreme!

— Babatunde Olatunji

Mac and I take a "practice pack" today. We pack our backpacks and are out of the house by 9:30 a.m. heading to Soberanes. Fog everywhere. We decide to start the 4.5 mile loop on the Rocky Ridge trail. Up, up, up. A young man coming down tells us the sun shines at the top. The trail is rocky and slippery. Half of the way up we stop to shed our fleece pullovers. Mac's T-shirt drips soaked with sweat.

This is our first hike using our new retractable, adjustable, light-weight trekking poles. We bought a pair of them and we each use one. Mac is used to using a hiking stick, but I have to learn. Mac keeps instructing me to put my weight on it. I switch hands occasionally to give both arms the chance to learn.

Soon we walk out of the fog to embrace the clear blue sky. Wow! What a treat. As we reach the top and go inland heading east, the Santa Cruz mountains and Fremont Peak rise in the distance above the extensive fog bank crawling through the Monterey Bay. More wildflowers are blooming than I expected.

As we start the descent toward the redwood canyon, I become aware of the change in pole technique

161

going downhill compared to up.

"Don't be afraid to put your weight on it," Mac coaches. "That's what it's for. Don't drag it. Use it. Let it be a third leg."

It takes a while to catch on but soon I can't imagine walking without it. What a great tool it is, helping to take the impact off of my knees and catching me if I slip a bit.

When we get home I weigh my pack—27 pounds. I weigh 110 pounds now, so 35% of my body weight is 33 pounds.

> *A good rule of thumb when deciding on your load is to aim roughly for one-fifth to one-fourth of your body weight. You can increase this to as much as one-third as you grow stronger.*
> — Cindy Ross and Todd Gladfelter,
> *A Hiker's Companion*

> *Most people try to keep their packs within lower weight limits: 30 pounds for a woman (maximum 40 pounds) and 40 to 50 pounds for an adult male. How heavy a pack you carry depends, however, upon your physical condition and experience, the terrain to be covered, the length of the trip and the time of year.*
> — Dian Thomas, *Roughing It Easy*

> *The heaviest load the average person can carry with efficiency and enjoyment for a long day's walking seems to vary within rather wide limits, but a rough guide would be "up to one third of body weight for a man, perhaps one quarter weight for a woman — because of her muscle structure." . . . The only way to get used to heavy loads is to pack heavy loads . . . .*
> — Colin Fletcher, *The Complete Walker III*

Okay. I'll go with the last excerpt. Colin Fletcher is the master walker. One quarter of 110 pounds is 27½ pounds. The pack today was a relatively easy load to carry. I'm sure I could carry up to about 35 pounds without stress or much strain. Yes, it will take effort but I expect that.

> *People such as Himalayan Sherpas, who have toted huge loads all their lives, can carry almost their own weight all day long. And even a halfway-fit, fully citified man can pack a very heavy load for short distances, such as canoe portages. Again, people whom I trust implicitly talk of having to carry 80 or 100 pounds or even more on slow and painful approach marches of five or ten miles at the start of mountain-climbing expeditions. But this kind of toil is hardly walking, in our sense.*
>
> — Colin Fletcher, *The Complete Walker III*

I pack as lightly as I can. Some folks are obsessed by packing ultra-lite and trade camping comforts for ease on the trail. I'll gladly carry my Therm-a-Rest® rather than do without. I'm rather sensible about the whole thing and today, 27 pounds was a piece of cake (perhaps a pound cake). Mac weighs his pack, . . . 40 pounds. That translates to 17% of his body weight. (He's a big boy!) I'm just happy to be going *out there*. Ten days until we leave for Lone Pine.

July 10, Wednesday ◯v/c

Assume a virtue though you have it not.
> — William Shakespeare

Two nights ago, Mac and I sat in bed and finalized Whitney plans. We're leaving Tuesday, July 16 (a day earlier than I thought). We made reservations for site #9, July 16, two nights at Whitney Portal Campground, set at 8100 feet. We'll see how we do with the altitude. On July 18 (Day Three), we'll probably camp at Outpost Camp (we'll call this Plan A), 3.8 miles from trailhead and at 10,365 feet. If we feel okay, we have the option of continuing up the trail to Trail Camp (Plan B) at mile 6.3 and 12,039 feet. We'll see.

Day One — Drive to and camp at Whitney Portal Campground
Day Two—Acclimate

Plan A
<u>Day Three</u> – Thursday: Outpost Camp. (3.8 miles)
<u>Day Four</u> – Friday: Hike to Trail Camp (2.5 miles). Set up camp.
<u>Day Five</u> – Saturday: Hike to summit. Return to Trail Camp (9.4 miles)
<u>Day Six</u> – Sunday: Descend the mountain (6.3 miles) and drive home.

Plan B
<u>Day Three</u> – Thursday: Trail Camp. (6.3 miles)
<u>Day Four</u> – Friday: To the summit. Return to Trail Camp. (9.4 miles)
<u>Day Five</u> – Saturday: Descend. (6.3 miles) Camp at Lone Pine Lake, Whitney Portal or Lone Pine campground.
<u>Day Six</u> – Sunday: Travel day.

Plan C
<u>Day Three</u> – Thursday: Outpost Camp. (3.8 miles)
<u>Day Four</u> – Friday: Trail Camp, daypack to summit, return to TC (11.9 miles)
<u>Day Five</u> – Saturday: Descend (6.3 miles)
<u>Day Six</u> – Sunday: Drive home.

Plan A is a more relaxed pace. Plan B is my choice so we can get up there as soon as possible. What if we attempt Plan A, get close on Day Five but the weather does not allow us to continue? If we try Plan B, however, and for some reason don't make it up Friday, we still have Saturday to try again. And, of course, a lot depends on how both of us do with the altitude and the pack up. Plan C is available if the 2.5 mile hike from Outpost to Trail Camp is a piece of cake. We'll see. I'm so excited.

BACKPACKING CHECKLIST

Basic Items
water bottles
water filter
AquaMira®
maps
compass
knife
sunscreens
headlamp
extra batteries
duct tape
toilet paper & spade
rope/cord
trash bag (rain gear for pack)
mosquito netting
electrolytes
firestarters
whistle
trekking poles
camera
needle/thread

First Aid
first aid kit
bandages
insect repellent
limes
aspirin, Ibuprofen®
Neosporin®
providone iodine
tweezers
waterproof tape
mylar blanket
moleskin

Sleeping Gear
tent
sleeping bag
Therm-a-Rest®

Recreational Gear
book
notepad & pen
reading glasses

Clothes
shirt
pants
underwear
fleece pullover
down jacket
rain jacket
hat
gloves
long underwear
handkerchiefs
sleeping clothes
dirty clothes bag
small towel

Optional
snowshoes
bathing suit
long sleeve shirt
shorts
extra shirts
vest
solar battery charger
sleeping bag liner
gaiters
rain pants
sarong

Personal
toothbrush
non-fluoride toothpaste
floss picks
hydrogen peroxide
hairbrush
wash cloth
body lotion
witch hazel
night cream
Q-Tips®
lip balm
CALM®
nail clippers
contact solution
contact holder
eye drops

Feet
hiking boots
socks
liner socks
camp shoes

Cooking
pots
dish towel
spoon
stove & windscreen
fuel
extra zip-lock bags
cup
matches (waterproof)
lighter
trash bag

Food
tea
oatmeal
almonds
GORP
cup-o-soups
energy bars

Misc.
cell phone
daypack
star chart
animal tracks chart
bandana
binoculars
scales
field guides

CAR CAMPING ADDITIONS

Basic Equipment
Coleman® stove/fuel
griddle
lantern/extra mantles
dishes & silverware
paper towels
table cloth
beach chairs
coffee cone & filters

After Trail Bag
shampoo/conditioner
clean clothes
shoes/socks
deodorant
towel
razor
quarters for showers
incense

Ice Chest (for car travel)
juice
rice milk
smoked turkey
mustard
lettuce
tomato
green onions
hummus
salsa

Miscellaneous
binoculars
playing cards
field guides
blanket
inner tubes

Picnic Basket
cutting board
bagel knife
butter knife
spoons
travel cups
bottle/can opener
extra zip-lock bags
bagels
bread
almond butter
brown rice cakes
cereal
agave
fruit
garlic
coffee
tea

July 12, Friday ○ Ⅱ

The mountains are calling and I must go.
— John Muir

Running around getting supplies together: Limes, energy bars, advance play lottery tickets, . . . you know, the important things. From the library I check out John Muir's book, *My First Summer in the Sierra*, again, to take with me. As I walk from the shelf toward the checkout desk, another book catches my eye: *Home to the Wilderness – A Personal Journey*, by Sally Carrighar. I open the book to a black and white photo of Sequoia National Park and instantly decide to take the book home. I've never heard of Carrighar or the book but it feels so right. Thank you. We'll have two days to read: Tuesday (travel day) and Wednesday (acclimation day). Of course we can read the other days on the trail, but I'll have to find a small, lightweight, paperback, rather than a hardcover.

July 14, Sunday ○♋

Like most other things not apparently useful to man, it has few friends, and the blind question, "Why was it made?" goes on and on with never a guess that first of all it might have been made for itself.
— John Muir, *My First Summer in the Sierra*

Muir was referring to poison oak. I read the quote aloud to Mac reminding him of our discussion while sitting around the campfire at Chain Lakes last year, surrounded by mosquitoes. "Everything has a purpose. But what possible purpose could there be for mosquitoes?" Mac holds that "mosquitoes are food. That's it."

Time for a "practice pack." As we load the car, our friend Dan drives up. Beth, his girlfriend, writes the music column for a local weekly newspaper. She's on her weekly deadline. Usually she works at home on Sundays and Dan goes for hikes. We tell him where we're going and invite him to join us.

We hike from the Saddle Mountain campground in Carmel Valley, to the top of Saddle Mountain, maybe one, maybe two miles up. I'm packing 35 pounds, that will probably be the maximum weight I'll carry up the Mount Whitney trail. It feels good. This trail (actually a dirt road) offers a steady, gradual climb. We talk and tell camping, backpacking, and hiking stories.

A hawk flies above us and we try to identify its kind. As Mac and Dan quit watching and walk on, my vision shifts from the hawk to something beyond the bird that looks small, shiny, white and round. It doesn't move. I don't see a jet trail. I stop the boys and point it out. It's very small. I lose sight of it and almost don't find it again. The boys can't find it at all and leave me standing. I watch. It doesn't move. I look down briefly and when I look up to try to find it again, I can't. Maybe it was a weather balloon. Maybe a UFO. It was cool!

The pack feels good. I'm ready to try it at the high elevations.

After the evening entertainment, Mac and I shop for food that we'll take on the trip. I am such a picky eater and Mac is so sweetly patient with me. *No MSG, sugar, or animal products. No hydrogenated anything, no yeast extract, no modified corn starch.* He reads all of the labels with me. I feel kind of bad like I'm a bother. He manages to say, once or twice, "That's what I like about going with the boys; they'll eat anything." I'd probably eat anything too, if that's all there was. But at this point I have a choice.

July 15, Monday ☽♋ (new moon)

Real generosity toward the future lies in giving all to the present.
— Albert Camus

I've got plenty to do today: Packing, laundry, errands, deliveries, eat, repair my pack, etc., . . . the usual things-to-do list when you're going to go climb Mount Whitney. Mac says we can leave late tonight or early in the morning.

Aja is not happy with me tonight. I gave money to the people who will be taking care of her for the next week but I didn't give her any. I didn't have it to give. I drop her off at Sara's, who she'll be staying with for the next six days. Aja gives off the air that she could care less that I am going away for a week to climb the highest peak in the contiguous USA. I let her go. Then, as she knocks at Sara's door, I call her back. "I hope you'll have fun this week. You are so loveable. I'm sorry that I can't give you some money. I love you." I wish that I could give her everything. She gives me a hug and a kiss.

Jeremiah will be here at home alone and working.

Mac and I stay up late doing finishing details: Checklists, ice chest, phone calls, dishes, cat box, pack the car, etc. We get to bed after midnight.

July 16, Tuesday ☉♌
Mount Whitney ~ Day One

From the summit of Mount Whitney only granite is seen. Innumerable peaks and spires but little lower than its own storm-beaten crags rise in groups like forest-trees, in full view, segregated by cañons of tremendous depth and ruggedness.

— John Muir, *The Mountains of California*

3 a.m. – I weigh in at 111 pounds FSI (from the skin in). My pack isn't packed all the way, so I can't weigh it. On the road by 3:30 a.m., to Highway 101. The morning light starts peeking through the fog as we get closer to Paso Robles.

5:15 a.m. – I take over driving at Paso Robles and drive east on Highway 46. Anticipation of the sunrise awakens my senses. Fog begins to clear halfway to Highway 99. Shades of gray are slowly replaced by golden grass and green trees. In the distance the silhouette of the majestic Sierra patiently awaits the new day. My excitement builds in anticipation of the sun rising over the Sierra.

5:55 a.m. – A subtle red glow ignites behind the glorious Sierra skyline. Rays of red begin to shoot outward from the still hidden rising star. I tingle all over. The surrounding land is flat but my perfect view is soon obstructed by seemingly endless rows of almond trees. I drive quickly, hoping to get beyond the orchards. A reprieve arrives just in time to see the red fire of the glowing star.

"Wake up, honey. You've got to see this."

Mac had been far away in slumber and arrives back half asleep.

I find a spot to pull over. We take a moment to pay homage to the gift of light from the Universe.

7 a.m. — The world is awake. We pass through Bakersfield, turning east on Highway 178. Not much traffic for a work day.

Away from the city, the familiar citrus groves line the southern entrance to the Kern Canyon. I recall last year, on our trip to the Upper Kern River, a hot afternoon in April, the orange blossoms filled the air with a fragrance as sweet as heaven. Ah-h, aroma therapy. Driving into the canyon, the Lower Kern gushes through the boulder garden; waterfall and rapid tumble one after another. Mount Whitney water flows into the Kern. I look for boats then declare this section unrunnable. *Too high. Too fast. Wouldn't do it.* The road winds with the river, snuggling close to the canyon walls. Turn after turn, rocks jut out close to fenders, headlights and bumpers. The sky is clear, the air is warm. A perfect day.

Miles ahead, Kern River Road turns as we cross the river. The highway divides and grows into a swifter, straighter four lane freeway compared to what we have left behind. In no time we are at Lake Isabella, a reservoir. I'm not fond of reservoirs. I imagine all that was submerged under water in the name of human desire, growth, and *improvements*. Let's stay small. We're guests here on this planet. Why can't we treat it with more respect?

8:15 a.m. — I'm getting tired. We stop at the small store in Onyx, where I bought some local honey last April. Buckwheat honey. I ask Mac to drive. He does. I try to sleep, but can't. I'm not sure Mac is wide awake yet.

We drive past the Scodie Mountains to the south and up to Walker Pass. The Pacific Crest Trail (PCT) crosses the highway here. Over the pass, Joshua trees reign. The Inyo Mountains sit far away to the east. We take Highway 14 north to 395. Now I'm too excited to sleep. I try to meditate and manage to clear my mind briefly of all thoughts, but I don't slip over to the other side, receiving too many incoming thoughts. I resign my Self to wakefulness. I pull out maps, trying to identify the peaks, canyons and creeks to our west. We'll be in Lone Pine soon.

9:40 a.m. – We're here. Lone Pine. Mount Whitney glows with majestic grandeur. We're home. There's the visitor's center, Gardiner's Sport Store, Kirk's Barber Shop and the grocery store. Breakfast. It's time to eat. We cruise the main street surveying our options. We choose the restaurant with two California Highway Patrol cars parked out front and a full parking lot.

We take a four top and I sit next to Mac so we can both look out at the eastern Sierra. The couple next to us speaks in German. The man gives his order to the waitress in excellent English. After we order, I lean over and start a conversation. Mac says to ask questions that you know the answer. But I wasn't absolute what their reply would be. "Where are you from?"

"Germany," the man says.

"What part? . . . not that I've ever been there . . . ." They tell me but I can't repeat their reply. "Your English is very good."

"Ah," the man shuns the compliment. "Thank you."

"Where did you learn to speak so well?"

"I play basketball with some Americans. They taught me."

I note some northern U.S. accent, like Wisconsin or Minnesota but I don't pursue that line of questioning. "Where are you going?"

"Yosemite, San Francisco. Then we're going down Highway 1 back to Los Angeles," the man does all the talking.

"Oh. We're from Monterey."

No sign of recognition on their faces.

"Carmel, Big Sur . . . ? It's lovely. You'll go right through the area. We left there at 3:30 this morning."

He looks at his map as a look of shock and surprise passes his face. "We left Death Valley at 7:30 this morning. We got there yesterday, in Badlands at 5 p.m. No one was there. We watched a beautiful sunset all alone."

"How long have you been here in the United States?" passing time as we all wait for our food.

"A week and a half."

"In Los Angeles?" Now I am surprised.

The woman says quickly, "No. We've been to the Grand Canyon, to Phoenix and San Diego. I liked San Diego. It's so beautiful."

"And warm," I add. Living in Monterey, I often forget what the hot summer sun feels like.

"In Phoenix, we were very lucky. We heard that the Dream Team was in town. We went to the arena to buy tickets but they were sold out. We waited in line until after the game started. They said they might have some seats that were unsold. Fifteen minutes after the game had started we got two tickets. We sat in the front row. I couldn't believe it."

"You were lucky," Mac perks in.

Our food arrives and silence ensues.

After grub guzzling and waiting for the bill, I ask the foreign pair, "What has impressed you most about being here?"

"The road signs here come up so fast. There's not enough warning. We miss our turns. In Germany the roadways have signs every ten meters. You can't miss them." They look at each other. "Hm. The driving. People don't drive so mean and fast. On the autobahn in Germany, you can drive fast, 200 miles per hour, if you want. And you can only pass on the left. If someone is driving in the left lane and they're going slower than you want to go, you can't pass them. People get angry, but they cannot do anything about it. They sometimes pass on the right but they have to pay big money if they get caught.

"Also the roads are so wide here. Maybe it's because the American cars are so big. We have narrow roads."

We chit chat a little then I ask what I really want to know: "What is the weirdest thing you've noticed here?"

"Weird?" The man looks at his partner's face. She doesn't understand the word *weird*. He translates *weird* to her in German, "schlimmste."

I bump in, "How do you spell that? No, let me guess." (I dig deep into the files of junior high school days with Frau Hett and Herr Ahern, "S-C-H-L-I-M-S-T-E."

"Close! S-C-H-L-I-M-M-S-T-E. Good. One more M," the man returns.

"Unusual. What's the most *unusual* thing that you've noticed," I ask looking at the lady. I want to encourage her to participate in the conversation.

"Good bookstores," the man says. "Where are the good bookstores?"

I nod in sympathy.

"What kind of books?" Mac enters.

"Sport books," the foreign tourist answers eagerly.

"San Francisco," Mac offers. "You should be able to find a few good bookstores in San Francisco."

We all talk a bit more then the waitress brings their bill. Mac points to the man's fanny pack. It is made from basketball material, not like a basketball in size, but in material, color, texture, and markings. I comment to the man about it.

"I bought it in Germany."

We shake hands and say our good-byes.

11 a.m. – We drive the short way to the Lone Pine Visitor's Center. I remember their great book selection. It's very hot now, desert hot, *at least* 95°, probably higher. I call Miah at work to let him know that we arrived safely. Aja is

with Sara at her mom's beauty salon and I don't have that phone number. I hope she's okay. I didn't like our parting.

We spend a good hour going through the bookshelves. I eavesdrop on the tourists and ranger discussions and recognize the lady ranger we had talked with when we were here last year. The rangers patiently repeat directions and survival instructions to those whose destination is Death Valley. The rangers advise taking at least four liters of water per person. *[NOTE: Later I look up liter on a conversion table. Four liters = 4.23 quarts, or one gallon plus one cup. Why don't they say one gallon? Americans don't generally know how to convert. I don't without a conversion chart. Maybe most of their visitors are foreign and are more familiar with metric.]* Death Valley is 135 miles to the southeast and temperatures easily reach 100. It's not uncommon for the temperature to hit 120 this time of the year.

A young woman and two boys, who look to be about 12 and 14, enter. She asks the lady ranger, "What's there to do around here?"

"Well . . . ."

Before the ranger has the chance to reply, the woman continues, "We'll probably climb Mount Whitney first, then I thought, this afternoon, we'd go see Death Valley, and then . . . we'll be here three days. Is there an amusement park close by?" With the words *amusement park,* the boys start paying attention.

Another ranger pops in, "You can come to my house. That's pretty entertaining. What a circus."

The woman confesses, "I guess I've always wanted to see these things since I was a child, but my boys are kind of bored."

I stop listening to their conversation. I sense what the ranger wants to say but she handles it with grace and patience.

Mac finds a couple of good books: *Sequoia and Kings Canyon – The Official National Park Handbook* #145 and *The*

High Sierra – Peaks, Passes, and Trails by R.J. Secor. He also finds a photocopy of July's Star Chart that costs only 25 cents.

As we pay for our goods, I tell the ranger (the one that I recognize) that we won't ask her for directions anywhere. She sighs a big breath of relief. Then we tell her we are going to start our hike up Whitney on Thursday.

With a panicked look she asks, "Do you have your permit?"

"Yes. We were here last year and hiked halfway up to check out the trail. We applied for and got a Mount Whitney Summit Zone wilderness permit for four days. We don't want to do it in one day. We've both had bouts with altitude sickness so first we're going to camp two days at Whitney Portal Campground to acclimate then we'll take four days on the trail."

"I like people like you," she says.

"He's read all the books we could find. He's done his homework," I say motioning toward Mac.

"You wouldn't believe what people do. One van load of 22 people went to Death Valley with *no* water. Not one drop. They wonder why we tell them to bring extra water. They find out when their cars break down." She goes to the cash register. "You know what I'd do? I'd hike to Lone Pine Lake the first day and camp. Nobody camps there and it's so beautiful. I love it. Then I'd hike to Trail Camp the next day. Then I'd hike to the summit." She wishes us luck, advises us to start drinking plenty of water now, at least three quarts a day, and have fun. "Come back and tell us about your trip."

"We will."

12:30 p.m. – As we drive closer to Whitney Portal, our excitement grows. We had a dream. We planned. We studied. We took care of the details. We prepared. We trained. We're here. We drive past the Family Campground, where we assume our campsite is, and up to the end of the road to a turnaround. There's a small store (with T-shirts, souvenirs, snacks, and other things for sale), a stocked fishing pond, lots of parking, a gorgeous waterfall, a spectacular view of Mount Whitney and the surrounding peaks, and the Mount Whitney trailhead. How good it feels to be here. How beautiful the mountains are, . . . and how humbling.

"We're going to climb that," I state, not a question.

Driving back to the Family Campground, the view of Owens Valley to the east is equally breathtaking. We pause, feel the moment, then turn into the campground and cross a bridge. Lone Pine Creek gushes down the mountainside, hopping over boulders and fallen trees. "Not many people here," I expected more. We find #9 and a reservation sign greets us with *McDonald 7/16 thru 7/18*. We pull in and check out the campsite. Perfect. Two excellent tent sites, secluded but open, an easy walk to the creek and restrooms just across the bridge. Home. We're home. Shattered windshield glass sits scattered around our parking space. *Bears,* I sense.

We unload and set up our tent. I have a slight headache and we're both in need of sleep. As soon as camp is set up, we climb into the tent to take a nap. I feel dizzy as I hit the pillow. *Water. Drink water,* a little voice whispers. I drink. Soon we both become unconscious.

The sun comes out from behind a tree and beats on our tent, making it incredibly hot inside. I look over at Mac. He's shirtless. I unbutton mine and doze off again.

Soon the sun wins. We get up. It's late afternoon. We hike the trail that follows the creek up to the end of the road.

"Maybe tomorrow we can climb up the waterfall trail," I suggest.

As we cross through the parking lot we come to a backpacker leaning next to his car and unpacking.

"How was your trip?" I have to ask.

"Great. Just great. Have you been?" he returns.

"No. We're going up Thursday," Mac responds.

We talk a bit then the backpacker says, "Be sure to put all of your food in your trunk or hide it real good. A bear broke into my friend's truck parked right here the night before they were going to the summit and ate all of their food. He even ripped open a can of tuna. If you can, spray your car with ammonia. Bears don't like ammonia. It seems to keep them away." We talk a bit more then bid *adieu*.

Adults lounge in lawn chairs and throw their fishing lines into the little stocked pond hoping to catch the big one. Children run around playing tag and being kids. At the store a young man is mopping. We stop just inside the door noting the wet floor.

"Are you open?" Mac asks.

With a short hesitation he says, "Yeah, . . . we have some T-shirts and stuff in the next room," and tweaks his eyes and head in the direction behind him to his left.

We take the hint and stand still. We look at the floor. The young man looks too. The floor is mostly dry and he knows it. "Oh, come on in," resigning his hopes of closing early. He's still got another 45 minutes until closing time.

I worry about Aja and think about calling her. I left her in such a snit and I'd sleep better hearing her voice and knowing she's fine. "Is there a pay phone here?" I ask.

"Nope. No phone up here."

That settles that. Mac finds another map and I find some really cool sunglasses for $5. What a deal.

"Be sure to put all your food away. There was a bear here two nights ago," the young man behind the counter seems more entertained trying to scare rather than caution us.

"Do you have any ammonia for sale?" Mac asks.

"No, I don't."

As we leave the store and walk down the hill toward the Family Campground, I realize that the glasses change my depth perception. I rarely wear sunglasses but it might be wise to wear some sort of UV eye protection at the higher altitudes. With these glasses on I have trouble judging how far away the ground is. I play with my glasses for a bit, trip over my feet and laugh. Even though the canyon is now in the shadows, I wear the glasses. Practice.

When we return to campsite #9, it's dinner time! I whip out the Coleman® stove and begin. I love it out here. We have neighbors down the hill but they can't be seen unless we walk down to the edge of our campsite and peek over the rocks. What a lovely evening. Perfect weather; not one cloud in the sky. Warm, but not hot. Breeze, but not wind. I'm so happy to be here.

I have a kitchen visitor. A bird. A noisy, bold, gray bird flies down onto the table. I've never seen this kind before. It's aggressive, like a jay, but gray with black, beady eyes and black wings. I shoo it away. It sits up in the tree and watches, waiting for me to leave my post. It attacks the table again, swooping down for food. I wave my arms and let it know he's not welcome to eat our food. "Go eat some berries or grubs," I suggest. We should not encourage wildlife to seek out humans as a resource for food. I cook and keep a watchful eye on my new friend.

At dinner, we discuss plans for tomorrow. So far so good. We don't feel any sign of altitude sickness, but we are, after all, only at 8100 feet. We'll hang here tomorrow, then start up the mountain on Thursday. I retrieve *A Field Guide to Western Birds* and attempt to identify our friend. I don't find it and refer to the *Sierra Nevada Natural History* guide. "Here it is. The Clark's Nutcracker, page 258, right next to the Yellow-billed Magpie and the Stellar Jay: *The Nutcracker (Clark crow or "camp robber") is the most conspicuous bird of upper sun-drenched slopes.* I return to *A Field Guide to Western Birds: Near camps and picnic sites it begs and steals food scraps*. Duh! What a charming little pest. The Clark's Nutcracker."

After dinner I find the perfect kitchen spot and wash dishes. The warm, soapy water feels good. I pretend it's a whole bubble bath.

With the kitchen chores done and the food put away, we walk not far to the edge of the Family Campground and buy some firewood. My imagination wanders to the next few days, wondering of the adventures that may lie ahead.

Back at camp we build a fire and sit up for a while chit chatting under the stars. Mac reads for a bit but I'm eager to see tomorrow so I turn in. Mac soon follows. I meditate. He reads. How happy I am to be here in my sleeping bag, in a tent, at the foot of the great Mount Whitney. Thank you. Namaste.

July 17, Wednesday ○♌
Mount Whitney ~ Day Two

When we are not sure, we are alive.
— Graham Greene

I wake at the light of day. I didn't sleep well. I worried about the bears. I thought about the granite slabs that fell recently in Yosemite National Park, but quickly changed my mind to think of other things.

I toss and turn. I want to get up and take a walk, but I don't want to meet any bears who might still be out running around, doing bear things. I'll stay right here and meditate.

Nature calls. I have to get up. Another glorious day featuring a brilliantly blue, cloudless sky. *Oh welcome sun, bring us your light.*

In getting my morning things out of the car, dried dirt and paw prints on the car suggest that we had visitors. Mud spatters on the passenger side door (where a little broken glass still sprinkles on the ground from a previous break-in) and on the driver's side door. Nocturnal, prowling mammals pawed our car. No broken windows. No ripped off doors or trunk. We're lucky. The back windows are tinted, so perhaps that helped. When Mac gets up, I show him. We see where it tried to lodge its claws in the door separation, but didn't follow through.

The *camp robber* joins us for breakfast. After clean-up, Mac reads guidebooks and maps. I join him, but do more writing than reading. Then I find a nice spot in the sun and plant myself. I read. I write. We're occupied for hours.

After lunch we take our packs, clothes, food, gear, and equipment out of the car. Everything we intend to take up the mountain with us tomorrow. It's time to pack. We spread out everything on the picnic table and benches. Packing right is important and takes time. The weight has to be distributed comfortably. I repackage the remaining food in zip-lock bags. Food is divided up into separate breakfast, lunch, snack, and dinner bags. Water bottles. How many pairs of socks? How many T-shirts? Book? First-aid. The packing and repacking process takes a long time. We check and recheck our lists. Everything has to be perfect. It's no fun to be *out there* and say, "Gee, I forgot the . . . sunscreen, flashlight, . . . or whatever." We take our time and do it right. There's such a fine line between *not enough* and *too much*. I take the clothes I'm wearing, plus my fleece pants and pullover, underwear, socks, and a jacket. I'm wearing the same shirt and cut-offs for four days. I'm taking my rain gear (pants and jacket). I'll carry the stainless steel pots and pans (since I refuse to use aluminum and insist on using the heavier stainless steel) and the stove. Mac will carry the tent and the water filter. We'll split the food. We'll each take a daypack for the ascent to the summit. We've done all we can do today. The packing process takes much longer to do than to write about it.

A walk. I've waited all day for a walk. We should take a practice hike to see how we do at this altitude. We load our daypacks with water, map, rain gear, flashlight, compass, matches, my Swiss Army backpacking knife, sunscreen, some first-aid supplies and a couple of bagels. Weather can change quickly up here in the Sierra, and one should always be ready for anything. I even bring a piece of newspaper in case we need to start a fire.

We set off down the trail that goes to Lone Pine campground. It's 4+ miles downhill from here, but we choose not to do it all. Mac has read in the guidebooks about a good day hike on the Meysan Lake Trail. The Lone Pine Trail forks to the left and we go right, up a narrow paved drive. We walk through a neighborhood of summer cabins. I'd live here all winter if I could. I imagine how beautiful this place is in the wintertime. The Meysan Lake Trail is clearly marked. We leave the asphalt and cabins and set our feet to work. I run the checklist through my mind, thinking that being out here might help me realize any forgotten items for tomorrow. The recent rock slides in Yosemite Valley has certainly given these rock walls a new dimension in my reality. Rather than being stoical monuments, they've become living, changing elements of nature. I choose to ignore the idea that the overhanging rocks could fall at any moment. I hear running water down below. The trail cuts across the mountain horizontally about halfway between creek and peak. Looking backward, the view of Owens Valley brings a smile to my face. It feels so good to be out here. The trail, the rocks, the sky, the trees.

"Is this Lone Pine Creek?" I ask Mac when I catch up to him. "Does Lone Pine Creek come down from Meysan Lake or Mount Whitney?"

Mac gets the Tom Harrison map out of my daypack pocket. "Meysan Creek. Lone Pine Creek comes down from Mount Whitney Trail. There's a north and a south fork."

We pick up speed to get in as much trail as we can and to test our bodies in the higher elevation. So far so good. I must remember to breathe and drink water, plenty of water. At higher altitudes a person has to breathe more to receive oxygen but the body's fluids are released with each breath, so more water is necessary. I've got my lime slices to help keep the bugs away. Not a cloud in the sky. Excellent weather today.

We walk an hour or so and turn back. I'd like to walk on, but I listen to *O Practical One*. I'd walk to Meysan Lake and end up walking back to camp in the dark. We've still got the final packing to do and dinner. We'll get to bed early so we can get a fresh start up the trail early in the morning.

I feel dizzy, then remember to breathe and drink water. I definitely feel the difference up here regarding the breathing requirements. I'm so excited about tomorrow. I'm ready to go now.

We arrive back at campsite #9 with plenty of daylight left.

O Practical One speaks, "We should go into town and buy ice to fill up the ice chest for while we're gone. We could get some bread, . . . some extra batteries, . . . and ammonia for the car."

We go. Down, down, down. We drive past Lone Pine Campground into the tiny town of Lone Pine. It's late afternoon, five-ish and it's hot, real hot. July in the Owens Valley. I imagine what Manzanar would be like now. We get supplies except for ammonia. The grocery store has only lemon-scented ammonia on their shelf. We want the stuff that smells bad.

We drive down the road to try a mini-mart. Mac goes in. I stay outside seeing my opportunity to call Aja. I reach her. She had a wonderful day. The girls hung out all day in the hair and nail salon and had the works done to them. Aja was in heaven. She's such a girl. I am happy to make contact with her and to hear that she is having fun.

"We'll be starting up the mountain tomorrow morning."

"Have fun, Mom."

"Thanks. You too. I love you."

"I love you, too."

Mac carries out some beer and ammonia. We're ready. All systems go. We drive back up to Whitney Portal Campground and into campsite #9. Everything looks in good shape, except someone has been nibbling on my sponge. Probably that *camp robber*.

I cook dinner, trying to use up all the perishable food in the ice chest. Mac reads. We eat. I offer, "Can we set our goal low tomorrow? Say, . . . Lone Pine Lake?" The lake is only 2.5 miles up and I don't want to be disappointed if I get tired and don't make it too far.

"We'll see how we feel when we get there, okay?"

While doing the dishes in my baby blue plastic dish pan full of warm, sudsy water, I imagine tomorrow night. Where will we be? Will we have remembered the essentials? Will the weather hold? Will we be visited by bears? Will we be tired and sore? I've been over my checklist many, many times. I'm so eager to go I can't believe it.

While brushing my teeth, my eyes catch the colors in the western sky created by the setting sun. With toothbrush in mouth, I stroll up to the car to get the camera and a better view of Mount Whitney. Before I get a chance to unlock the door, I turn to see a group of campers up the road, looking and pointing into the woods. A man glances down the road towards me and points to behind the cabin across the road and yells, "Bear! It's coming your way!"

I look to see it, . . . and I do! *Dark reddish brown. Not as big as I thought a bear would be. Maybe it's a young one. If it is, the mother might be close behind.*

I run back to camp to get Mac. "Buh bur voh moo voo. Obu ba!" He can't understand a word I'm saying with the toothbrush in my mouth, so I hold up my arms, make claws with my fingers, and growl. I roll my eyes and tilt my head, trying to say, *Follow me.* He understands. I return to the road, Mac behind, but not close. I cautiously cross the road, keeping alert for The Bear. The young one reappears from behind another cabin further down. It may be full grown. It's not a baby. Keeping a sharp eye for other bears, I walk toward the bear, holding my arms up wide, so I look big and ferocious. I jingle the car keys, since I don't have a pot or pan to bang. I get closer. The bear turns and waddles the other way. I follow. Suddenly, it stops, turns around, stands up, and looks straight at me. A thought comes to my mind, *Wait a minute. What am I trying to do here? I'm trying to frighten a bear away. My own children aren't afraid of me. Whoops!* Action suspends for a brief moment as we make eye contact. My fear passes and the bear's fear returns. (S)he disappears into the woods.

"Bruh bruh bree bro?" I ask Mac. But he didn't see him. The fear of seeing a bear is now history. I've seen a bear, my first one, . . . and survived. I've read that Black Bears, unlike the great Brown or Grizzly Bears, are *relatively* harmless. But still, I felt anxious and worried about seeing one out here. Now that I have seen one I feel better.

I finish brushing my teeth and resume the sunset tour. Oh what a beautiful mountain. I can't wait. I can't believe we're going up there. What an awesome sight it is.

We secure our camp, being mindful of covering everything up in the back seat of the car that remotely looks like human food. With paper towels, we swab the car with diluted ammonia. We snuggle up together in our tent and try to sleep.

July 18, Thursday ☽ goes into ♍ at 11:16 a.m. (Saturn goes retrograde at 1:29 p.m.)
Mount Whitney ~ Day Three

The richest values of wilderness lie not in the days of Daniel Boone, nor even in the present, but rather in the future.
— Aldo Leopold

I wake with the sun to see Mount Whitney catch the first rays of light in the clear, blue sky. It's yet another gorgeous day in paradise.

Bear signs on the car but just on the passenger side. It looks like, from the muddy traces, it tried to wedge its claws in the space between door and roof again, probably to rip the door off. I've seen photos. Fortunately, and for whatever glorious reason, the car is not hurt, again. *Thank you, Universe.* Mac goes for a morning walk and comes back with tales that some child's backpack got ripped into.

I cook pancakes and we eat some more perishables. We repack our backpacks for the last time. *How did John Muir do it with just his overcoat and a pocket full of biscuits?* We load everything up and drive to trailhead parking. We unload, and put ice chest, picnic basket, and teal-colored plastic storage bin into the trunk. A group of men park nearby and empty all of their gear onto the asphalt. One comes over to ask about our trekking poles. We talk backpacking in the Sierra. They're rock climbers. They're going up the Mountaineer's Route that forks off from the Mount Whitney Hiking Trail.

Another man asks Mac to take a picture of their group of four by the trailhead sign. I talk to the climbers.

After fine tuning every last detail, we hoist our packs up onto our backs. Mine feels good; not too heavy. "I can carry more. Give me more weight."

"Just wait a while. It might get heavier sooner than you think," Mac speaks through lips of experience.

I listen.

A young lady in a simple, short, forest green, A-line dress and sweater, comes down the trail with two fun-looking dogs.

"Will you take our picture by this sign?" I ask her.

"Sure," and she does.

"Let the wild ruckus begin. Up, up, up." It's 8:30 a.m. Not 6 a.m., but still early enough to avoid the midday heat.

We pass through the lupine jungle. I remember it from last September but now, they're still buds, shoulder high, with just a few blossoms on the tops. Mac takes a picture of me lost in the lupine. Penstemon. White yarrow. Trees, rocks, water, flowers, blue sky, Mac, granite cliffs, a trail and a mountain. What more could I ask for?

At the second creek crossing, 0.8 miles up, we stone-step across the North Fork of Lone Pine Creek. The Mountaineer's Route forks cross-country straight uphill from here. We stay on the hiking trail. Soon, the *John Muir Wilderness* sign welcomes us. I feel great. The new trekking pole makes quite a difference. I've learned to send it out in front of my body, plant it firmly, place my body weight upon it, and pull myself into it. It's a third leg. When there's a high step, it really pays for itself. I plant it and pull myself up. I routinely change hands to keep a balance. I'd like to have two now.

We take a break every half hour. *Breathe deep,* I hear the little voice. I compare this physical exertion to birthing a baby, with this being much easier. In labor, I couldn't stop whenever I wanted, rest under the shade of a pine tree and take in the view of the Owens Valley. Again I offer to lighten Mac's load. He declines.

The Lone Pine Lake natural dam appears up the trail high above us.

"We'll lunch at the lake. Okay?" I say to let Mac know that my energy is fine and I am willing to hike on.

Down the trail comes a lone backpacker, a thin, efficient body, with a dark tan, well-worn boots and clothes that could probably stand up by themselves. Mac stops and asks, "Did you go to the summit of Mount Whitney?"

"Yes, and the John Muir Trail from Tuolumne Meadows. Twenty days, . . . ten days were play. I'm a rock climber. My wife made a food drop at Florence Lake and was supposed to join me for the rest of the trip but she had to work. I have done this trip every year for nine years. Last night I spent the night alone on the summit of Mount Whitney. Yesterday a 76-year-old woman hiked to the summit. It was her birthday. I was watching her then she said, 'Oh, what the heck . . .' and she prepared to do a headstand. I asked her to wait so I could get my video camera. She was amazing."

This morning he hiked down from the summit, 4.7 miles, to Trail Camp, without any food or water. No breakfast. He said it was brutal. He got water at Trail Camp. We offer some food then I ask, "What was your favorite part?"

His head tilts and his face makes a funny look. I can see the memories spinning like a slot machine. Then something comes to mind, "Sleeping on the summit last night. The stars, the sky. Watching the sunset, then watching the sunrise, from the summit," he glows with a smile that covers his face.

Oh I wish to know that joy. We walk on. I dream of being out here for 30 days, from new moon to the next. My imagination wanders but my eyes keep a mindful look on the trail. This is no time to walk carelessly. Awareness is crucial to avoid accidents and still enjoy the sites. And what wonderful sites they are. The morning sun warms and feels good.

The second backpackers to come down the trail are a man and a young boy, who looks to be about 12 years old. I stop them and ask, "What was your favorite part?"

Without hesitation the man replies, "This part, right here. Going down."

The look on my face invites an explanation.

He continues, "We got real sick up at Trail Camp. The altitude got us. It's nice to be down here."

"When did you start hiking?" Mac asks.

The child doesn't speak. The man continues, "Yesterday morning. We hiked all day and got to Trail Camp at about 4:30. We felt real bad. We set up our tent, got inside and stayed there all night. We couldn't even fix or eat dinner. I came out once, quickly saw Candlelight and went back to the tent. Candlelight is amazing. You'll see it. Where are you camping tonight?"

"Outpost Camp," Mac answers.

"That's smart. You'll have the chance to get used to the altitude." The child still doesn't say a word. I don't think he is having much fun. He has a nice, new wooden walking stick.

"Did you hike to the summit?" I ask.

"No way," the man answers. "We couldn't wait to get back down here. This is beautiful. I felt so bad up there. I would have given anyone $100 to carry my pack down for me."

We laugh and say our good-byes. I'm finding it interesting talking to those who have been there. I'm curious to know where I'm going and what I'm getting myself into. I'm surprised how my otherwise shy self has become bold enough to initiate conversation with total strangers. But another backpacker feels like a kindred spirit. You have to love it to have gotten this far with a pack.

We stop to take advantage of the shade under a large pine. I smell it to see if it's one of those butterscotch smelling pines. It is!

"What kind of pine is this again?" I ask my walking RAMpack.

"Jeffrey Pine."

We hurry on, eager to see more.

The next backpacker we meet coming down, answers my question, *What was your favorite part?*, with an odd look.

"The whole mountain. I loved being up there." He had camped up at Trail Camp last night, six miles up.

"How cold did it get?" I ask, not fond of the cold.

"Triple layer. Once the wind picked up we got cold. But we survived." The other people he is with are lagging behind. "It's bleak up there, like the moon," and he continues walking down the trail.

At Lone Pine Lake, the trail cuts off and goes down to the lake or continues on. We count at least ten backpacks propped up against the rocks. Some probably belong to the hikers before us that we let pass. Some folks sit down by the lake. This year new regulations have gone into effect for the Whitney trail. Dayhikers can go this far without a permit. If they wish to go further, they are required to obtain a Day Use Permit from the ranger station.

"Hungry? What time is it?" I ask.

"10:30. I'm okay."

"Time for a snack? Apples?" looking forward to lightening my load. "Shall we keep going and eat our apples while we hike? We can get to Outpost Camp and pick out a good spot before all of those backpackers at Lone Pine Lake get up the trail," we grin and think ourselves quite clever.

I love the little forest in this part of the trail. It feels magical and enchanted. The trail climbs steeply from Lone

Pine Lake, up a rocky ledge, switchbacking. I press on, grunting on some of the step ups. Up, up, up.

About an hour later, the view opens onto Bighorn Park, a wide open spot nestled up against Thor Peak. Down. We cross the rocks and logs. Mac's boots are waterproof; mine are not. A roaring waterfall in the distance announces Outpost Camp, 3.8 miles from trailhead. Oh, . . . the flowers, ...

Outpost Camp. We're alone. Not a tent nor a human being to be seen. We survey the land and find a lovely spot with a perfect tent site that gracefully faces east, nestled near a granite wall, and features a perfect bear bag tree. Plus, in our backyard, a tumbling waterfall. Home. We're home. 11:20 a.m.

[NOTE: Bear-resistant food canisters are now required for overnight stays in the Mount Whitney Zone of Inyo National Forest.]

I smile, "Is there a cat-that-ate-the-canary grin on my face?"

After setting up the tent and the kitchen, we eat lunch. A little brown bird with red-streaked feathers wanders around rather boldly close to our feet. "We can't feed you. You have to stay wild." I look at my natural three-seed bread, with my all-natural, organic peanut butter and 100% fruit preserves, and toss a couple of crumbs. Mac tosses a huge piece of pretzel. "That's an afternoon project," I say.

People start arriving. They stop, eat lunch, walk to the waterfall, visit the solar latrine and then walk on. This is such a beautiful spot! It's 2.5 miles up to Trail Camp from here with more than a 1600 foot elevation gain. Mac and I both feel slight headaches. Elevation here is 10,365 feet. Enough hiking for today. Sunrise should be incredible from here. The Inyo Mountains stand magnificently in the distance across the Owens Valley.

I tend to wear my rose-colored glasses and not see things that I don't want to see but I have to note that the wooden building housing the solar latrine looks very out of place up here in this gorgeous wilderness. It's a tall structure, I suppose so the mechanics can be under the floor yet above the ground. It's necessary for the crowds of people who go up and down this trail every day.

Hey! There's something hanging in that tree. I walk over to check it out. It appears to be a huge, abandoned food bag, more like a duffel bag. Also up on a branch is a plastic, collapsible five-gallon water bag, half full. They seem to have been there a while. I'm not quite sure what to think and can only guess the scenario that lead to this arbor concoction. I go back to the tent and write some notes while Mac filters water at the creek and explores our new home.

I talk to a group of newly-arrived backpackers. One is a doctor, the others are registered nurses all from the same hospital. All but one are taking some kind of pills to counteract or prevent altitude sickness. I show them the abandoned bear bag and we discuss the how and why of it getting left behind. They're just stopping for lunch. They plan to camp at Trail Camp tonight.

Many other dayhikers and backpackers pass through. It's not till the end of the day that tents start popping up.

Early dinner. Pasta night. Mac has two chicken pasta cup-of-soups. I have tomato basil pasta soup. We also eat some vermicelli with olive oil and roasted garlic. I add some extra sun-dried tomatoes. A young man in a ranger uniform, carrying a shovel, walks over to our camp while I'm cleaning up dinner. He offers information about hanging our food so the bears won't get it, and instructs us not to take any food or scented items into our tent. He goes through the list – lip balm, sunscreen, gum, etc., . . . that I've heard before. I let him talk; it's his job. He tells us that there's a regular bear up here at Outpost, for the first time in years. He comments that it looks like we're doing a great job keeping our tent site clean and thanks us. I thank him and off he goes.

Mac tries the counter balance method to hang the food, that is always tricky and fun to watch. From the Sequoia & Kings Canyon National Parks publication, *Backcountry Basics*:

Last choice: Hanging food from trees

Use the counterbalance method only when storage boxes or canisters are not available. It is hard to do well, requires trees and rope, and bears can often thwart it. Reinforce this method with a human guard.

[Next there's an illustrated, six-step description]:

1. Find tree with a live, down-sloping branch, even if you must select a different campsite. Divide food into two balanced bags.

2. Use enough rope to go over branch and back to ground. Toss as far out on the branch as will support the food but not a cub.

3. Make sure no objects are below the branch that could support a bear. Tie on and hoist first sack up to branch.

4. Tie second sack high on rope; put excess rope in sack, leaving loop out for retrieval.

5. Toss or push lower sack up with stick until sacks are at equal height, at least 5' below the branch.

6. Retrieve with long stick through loop. Pull slowly to avoid tangles.

Mac extends his trekking pole to its limit and pushes one bag up. He ties the second bag onto the other end of the rope and pushes it way up out of our reach. It's up there. We'll see if it works *and* if we can retrieve it.

As the daylight nears its end, dayhikers wander down from above. I recognize some of the groups who walked by earlier on their way up.

We go to tent at eight o'clock. The sunset won't be visible from here and we'd have to do some extensive climbing to reach a spot where we could see it, so we turn in early. I read *Mount Whitney – The Trail Route,* a 6-page booklet published by Sierra Nevada Peak Guides, that includes the history, how to prepare for the climb (a little late for that), regulations, reservations, maps, guides, altitude, water, lightning, the trail (an aerial photo, a map) and a caution: *This publication is not a substitute for correct training, knowledge, good judgment or common sense. All climbers and hikers are responsible for learning techniques that ensure their safety in the mountain environment.* Not bad for $1.89. Mac is reading *Way Out Here – Modern Life In Ice-Age Alaska* by Richard Leo. Sometimes he chuckles. He occasionally shares, reading passages aloud so I can chuckle too.

It's only 8:30. If I get eight hours of sleep I'll be up at 4:30 a.m. Hm-m-m. I lay down to meditate, say a prayer and give thanks.

Time passes as thoughts enter my awareness and exit. However, one thought stays: "Today is July 18, isn't it?"

"Yes," Mac mumbles without missing a paragraph in his book.

"It's Hunter S. Thompson's birthday. I'll bet he's out celebrating right now."

Mac smiles and agrees.

Fear and Loathing on Mount Whitney. I can't imagine Hunter S. enjoying what we did today. I picture him hiking up the trail, smoking, complaining vigorously about the weight of his pack and wondering why we're doing this at all.

No radio? What do you do out there? Bugs? Snakes? Don't they get in the tent? What do you do all day? Are we there yet? [cough-cough] Can I have a drink now?

No, I can't imagine him here and I hope he has a wonderful birthday, wherever he is.

Okay. It's six minutes to nine. Maybe I'll try to meditate again. Good-night. Namaste.

July 19, Friday ☽ ♍
Mount Whitney ~ Day Four

One touch of nature makes us all kin.
—— William Shakespeare

Awake with the light of dawn. I peek out. Bear bag is okay. I unzip, get out and walk around. I'm the only one up. Mount Thor glows pink reflecting the morning sun. I wake up Mac. He grabs the camera and runs off to capture the morning glory. What a beautiful morning it is. Not a cloud in the sky. More tents are scattered around. More than were here when we went to tent last night.

After a quick, easy breakfast, we break down camp and pack up. I thank Outpost Camp for such a lovely spot. It's still a bit chilly, but I stuff my fleece pullover into my pack, sure that I'll warm up quickly once we start walking. We leave at 7:30 a.m. Only 2.5 miles to Trail Camp with an elevation gain of 1600 feet. There's nothing else I'd rather be doing. This is it.

A foursome passes us. Dayhikers. Soon a single dayhiker, moving quickly, passes. He's carrying a bagpipe. My eyes light up. *A concert?* Wouldn't that be splendid? He leaves us behind.

Soon we reach Mirror Lake, mile 4.3. Because of overuse, they've closed it to camping since 1972. I can see why people would want to camp here. We hurry on. Up, up, up. I spot the bagpiper. He's taking a break, sitting alongside the trail, catching his breath.

"Where are you gonna play?" I ask.

In an Irish or Scottish or some other accent, he responds, "Not sure. I'll see when I get there. I'd like to get to the summit."

I wish him luck and walk on. We reach the spot where we turned around when we dayhiked up here last September. I pause to recall the thought I had at that time, *I wish we were hiking to the summit.* A dream come true. I thank the powers that be. I thank Mac. The bagpiper passes us again. I hurry to stay close on his tail.

Five miles up and The Last Tree welcomes us to the High Country. Now comes the moonscape. Up, up, up. Slowly, steadily, we plod on. I feel a slight head throb and pop a couple of aspirin, drink more water, and slather some sunscreen on my arms and legs.

Trailside Meadow is in full bloom with purple Sierra Shooting-stars on a bed of green. White snow banks cover the north facing slopes. Thawed ice, trickles down the low spots. We snap a couple of pictures and move on, eager to get to Trail Camp. We pass the bagpiper, who sits resting on a rock. Up. Step after step. The weight of my pack is noticeable. I happily work at it, enjoying the effort to reach the result, at all times aware to be cautious. *This is no time to strain or sprain. Pay attention. It's okay to go slow. Be safe.* The internal conversation keeps me company. The bagpiper passes me again. I set my sights on him and follow. I don't want to miss the concert.

We reach a level area and overlook a beautiful lake nestled into the granite walls, restrained and cuddled by a natural dam, water as deep blue as the sky, . . . an unbelievable blue.

The bagpiper stops. "This is it. I'm not going any further," he declares with his slight accent. He lays his

195

bagpipe on a rock and takes off his daypack. "I'll have to catch my breath first."

I welcome the opportunity to take a break. "Do you mind if we stay for the concert?" I ask.

The bagpiper responds positively, so Mac and I drop our packs and lean them against a rock wall. Plenty of rocks up here.

The bagpiper begins to tune his instrument. "This is going to sound awful, for a bit, until I get it right." He returns to his bagpipe and, yes, the sound that comes out of it is not music, but still, it's pleasing to sit up here at over 11,000 feet, and listen to this otherwise foreign sound to the wilderness. I wonder if this lake has ever heard the bagpipes played before. I pull out the trail guide. Consultation Lake. It's so incredibly blue, deep blue. I'll bet it's freezing cold too. Mac gets the camera and begins taking pictures. I unpack a snack and start to nibble. Two men, one with a huge video camera, walk down the trail. I ask them, "What was your favorite part?"

"The summit," they both answer. After a few more words, they walk on.

The bagpiper finishes his tuning. In his accent he talks to himself, "Okay. Now I've got to do this right." He lays down the bagpipe and rustles through his daypack pulling out a kilt and some accessories, that I don't know their proper names. A young couple hikes down the trail then stops. The concert is about to begin.

"Would you take some pictures of me? I'm playing up here for my father. Yesterday I climbed to Telescope Peak in Death Valley and played. I want to give pictures to my father," he says as he holds out his camera to Mac.

Of course, Mac accepts. "Mac. My name is Mac. What's yours?"

"Tom," and he starts to play. A few notes into the tune and my spirit recognizes the song before my ears do. Tears well. *Amazing Grace*. My nose and heart tickle. I'm glad I have my sunglasses to hide the tears that are about to flow. This is the best. My heart sings as Tom plays. *How lucky I am. Thank you, Universe.* Mac takes pictures. I cry. I'm glad to have my hanky. Tom plays and walks over to the cliff overlooking Lone Pine and the Owens Valley. What a scene. My heart bursts open with JOY.

Closing *Amazing Grace,* Tom invites requests. Another couple has joined the audience. We let Tom choose his tunes. He plays. I remember the panoramic camera and shuffle through Mac's pack to find it. I snap a few pictures. I glance over to my pack and a ground squirrel is helping itself to the pretzels.

Tom plays a few more tunes, then claims no more breath and quits. The audience breaks into applause.

"What a treat. Thank you, Tom. Where did you learn to play?" I ask.

"I grew up in a Scottish apartment compound in Toronto and hung out with the old-timers. They taught me."

Mac thanks him too, takes his address and gives a promise to send pictures.

I'm in awe. *Who woulda thunk?*

The young couple comes over to talk. They're from Colorado. They tell of a musical festival where, at the end, one musician began playing *Amazing Grace.* Then, one-by-one, all of the other musicians joined until the stage was full. "What a feeling," they say.

I ask, "How's the trail up to Trail Camp?"

"This last stretch up there is the hardest. From there on it's a *piece of cake.*"

(Hey! Those are my words.)

I talk to another young couple from Vancouver. The lady had hiked to the summit a couple of weeks ago. This trip she plans to stay at Trail Camp while her boyfriend hikes to the summit. We all thank Tom and say good-bye. I still can't believe it. What a treat. A gift.

Marmots peek at us from behind rocks. They remind me of the Ewok characters in the *Star Wars*® movie.

We reach Trail Camp at 11:05 a.m. The sky has gotten a deeper blue. I didn't think it was possible. I have never seen a sky this dark blue. I hold my blue jacket up to the sky comparing realities. My mind knows the color of my jacket and I want to see if I'm hallucinating; it must be the altitude. The colors appear to be the same, . . . and still, not a cloud in the sky. It's a good day.

No problem with altitude. We both feel fine. 12,000 feet. The solar latrine greets us first. Then campers, all set-up. Perhaps they are hiking to the summit today. Lots of tents. Many of the tent sites feature human-made windbreaks, built with rocks. I'm guessing that it can get quite windy up here at night. The majority of the windbreaks block the west end of each campsite. There's no wind now, but we should take that into consideration in choosing a tent spot. The main trail offers some vacancies but I'd like a little more privacy. Mac takes off to scout the west end of Trail Camp. I scout the east end. A small lake, surrounded by melting snow pockets, nestles the rocks to the north. Mount Muir. Keeler Needle. Is that Mount Whitney?

A chilly wind blows sporadically down the mountains from the west. I find a great spot, over a small rock ridge, isolated from the main trail yet close to water. Mac is far away at the west end. I'm hesitant to drop my pack and leave it; the scoundrel marmots peek out from behind rocks, waiting for just that. But I don't want to leave the spot unclaimed. Another camper, looking for the perfect site, might claim this spot for his/her own. I drop my pack, climb the rock ridge, and wave my trekking pole to be noticed. He doesn't see me. I walk back to check my pack and re-evaluate the site. I take a wind check. The tent site is completely sheltered from the westerly wind. This is a good site. A naturally wind-shielded kitchen is already in place.

I leave my pack at the site and go far enough to see Mac wandering around the little pond but not far enough that I can't jump in to discourage the curious marmots. Mac wanders back and we discuss the pros and cons of this site. Hikers pass by down on the trail heading up or stopping here to camp. This site is close to the trail and the latrine but still, because of the rock berm, it's hidden and secluded. The pond is a short walk and we have a great view of the eastern sky, Mount Whitney and the famous Mount Whitney Trail Switchbacks to the west. Some references say 96 switchbacks and some say 97. We'll see tomorrow. Mac drops his pack and pulls out his binoculars. His attention focuses for some time and then, "See that little shadow way up on top between those rocks? That's a person."

I don't see it. I don't see anyone up there.

Mac hands the binoculars to me.

"Oh my goodness. That little, bitsy dot is a person?" That rock wall is tomorrow's new acquaintance. Hopefully, we'll all become friends. "Oh my goodness."

We set up camp and nibble on trail mix. I make some peanut butter sandwiches, a yummy gourmet delight. Camp is good, set to catch the earliest possible morning sun. We won't see a sunset tonight but there should be a baby moon over the rock wall.

Mac pulls out his book, binoculars and Therm-a-Rest® onto a rock and positions himself to face the switchbacks, curious to observe and let other hikers lead his eye up the trail. And they do. Droves of hikers swarm by eager to climb our country's highest peak. It's easy to tell the dayhikers from the backpackers by their gear or lack of it. Mac invites me to take a look. The little people cross back and forth up the hill, few, very few are coming down.

They move slowly. I watch for a while trying to map all of the visible trail.

Mac shares his sandwich with a pair of little birds, Rosy finches. I remind Mac that we're not supposed to feed people food to the wild life. He smiles and offers them another bit. They take it out of his fingers. The little birds entertain him for a very long time.

Time for a rest/meditation/nap, whichever comes first. I settle into the tent, lie down and relax. Nice hike today. It is such a beautiful trail, an incredible place to be. *Thank you feet and body for bringing me up here.* I slide off into the blue yonder, ...

Beautiful spot here at Trail Camp. My left upper thigh has a little bruise from hoisting my pack to lift it up onto my shoulders. I wander over to Mac. The hikers and binoculars are still the afternoon's entertainment. He offers a look. Someone walks up at the top on the snow bank, moves off the trail ignoring the switchbacks and goes straight down the snow chute. "Mac. Can you see that person?" I surrender the binoculars and Mac takes a look. "That looks dangerous," I observe. This impatient soul bypasses the designated trail and cuts the quickest and most dangerous way down. I hold my breath. He reaches a bottom and safely rejoins the trail. "Not me; no thank you. I'll stay on the trail." No one follows him.

Backpackers wander in and look for campsites. Nobody comes up to our side of the trail. I watch a group of young men, probably Boy Scouts, wander about, choose their campsite and begin to settle in. Mac watches all with the binoculars. The group claims a spot across the trail and up a bluff. They're close enough to see and guess what they might be doing but not close enough to hear.

Candlelight? What is Candlelight? I thumb through the Whitney literature looking for an answer. I find this:

Mile 6.3 (12,039 feet): TRAIL CAMP. . . . Most make an overnight stay here for beyond is the infamous climb to Trail Crest, that lies 1,738 feet above. There's a grueling series of 96 switchbacks to be overcome, and it's best to tackle this ordeal when well rested.
—Mount Whitney Guide for Hikers and Climbers

I read on still looking for Candlelight. I don't find anything in this book, the little chamber of commerce facts and information/map sheet, nor on the photo map. I could go out looking for Candlelight tonight but don't know what I'm looking for or where. Maybe it'll just show up. I'll keep my eyes open.

Across the canyon, a woman in a red sweatshirt socializes from tent to tent. She's wearing a very wide-brimmed straw hat, rather a bit much for out here but probably expresses her personality. Maybe she knows a lot of people up here or she's forgotten something and is going around trying to beg or borrow. Who knows? My imagination is entertained. The sound of her laughter travels all the way over here. Another straw hat catches my attention, . . . male, who seems to know the hatted woman.

The supposed Scout leaders gather the youngsters with backpacks and congregate on top of a rock overhang. Time for the hangings. Yellow-bellied marmots will gladly go through an abandoned backpack curious to find something to eat. I've read that marmots will chew on the backpack straps for the salt from sweat. Here, above the tree line, it is recommended to hang backpacks and food bags suspended off a rock wall by rope, out of reach of the marmots and, hopefully, the tiny squirrels that can climb up the sides of the rocks. The Scouts probably chose that bluff so they could take advantage of the slight elevation for this purpose. I watch the teachers. I'm not sure how they are trying to secure the ropes, but one, then another and more backpacks slide down the rocks to the ground. This may take a while.

On my way back from the latrine a woman approaches. We smile and greet each other. I let her know there's no vacancy at the moment and she starts to do some trail small talk and tells me, "I was just talking to a woman over there and her father is hiking with her. It's his seventieth birthday tomorrow and to celebrate the family is going to the summit of Mount Whitney. His name is Mr. Gee."

"Seventy? He's going to the summit?" I ask.

"Yes. This'll be his seventh time up; one for each decade. There he is, over there, in the straw hat."

I'm impressed and hope that I can hike to the summit of Mount Whitney when I'm seventy. I hope I can make it tomorrow!

Dinner is simple; veggie for me plus something animal for Mac. I eat less up here than I do when I'm home. We cook, clean and settle in for the evening show. A baby moon appears in the western sky just above the switchbacks and Trail Crest. We'll be up there tomorrow looking down. The sky continues to be crystal clear; no clouds. This is good.

I wrestle my Therm-a-Rest® out of the tent and sit on it in my sleeping bag on top of a rock. The last of the sun's rays leave our sight. The last of the peaks glow their fire red. Only the crescent moon to the west hints of our star's light. To the east, the Inyo Mountains silhouette the same fire-red glow. Where's Candlelight? Is this it? A pointy peak to the southeast glows a gentle red, maybe some days it could be bright as a candle. Beyond the mountains – darkness. From the east, Darkness approaches, . . . moving toward us. I've watched the morning light move in and take over as the Dawn but I've never seen Darkness move in like this. It's awesome, . . . amazing. I sit quietly and enjoy the show.

The Boy Scouts have given up on hanging the backpacks and instead have hung bear bags, or rather *marmot* bags, since bears don't usually come up here above tree line. Ten bags of green, blue, black, rust, yellow, white and two backpacks hang. Campers sit and stand around, watching night fall.

The crescent moon slowly dips lower, perched on top of a peak. Mount Muir watches over all. I feel safe, in good company. Grunts, groans, coughs, laughter, . . . a quiet, steady rumble of the little creek on the other side of the rocks. I shall sleep well tonight. We plan to get up at 5 a.m. and be on the trail ASAP. We'll watch the sunrise as we tackle the switchbacks up to Trail Crest. "Good-night Moon," I bid as it melts into the rock skyline. Does it get any better? No wind. It's perfect. The last light of the moon slips from my sight. A small mouse skitters around searching for crumbs. Do marmots come out at night?

I'm reminded of the summer when we were kids, that my brother Tom and I slept outside in the backyard almost every night under the starry or foggy sky. We often talked long talks, late into sleep time, inspired by the vast Universe. Although I don't remember what we talked about, I know it was deep, meaningful conversation, at least as deep and meaningful as children our age could muster. The dark, starlit night inspires wonder and awe.

I follow a few shooting stars and lie beneath the starry sky long enough to fall asleep, dreaming of tomorrow.

With the Milky Way now high overhead, I wake up with cold feet. My three-quarter-sized sleeping pad doesn't insulate my feet and legs from the cold rock. I pack up, move back into the tent and join Mac, who left his body hours ago.

July 20, Saturday ☾ ♍
Mount Whitney ~ Day Five

Now away we go toward the topmost mountains. Many still, small voices, as well as the noon thunder, are calling, 'Come higher, come higher.' Farewell, blessed dell, woods, gardens, streams, birds, squirrels, lizards, and a thousand others. Farewell, farewell.
—— John Muir, *My First Summer in the Sierra*

If anyone wonders if there's a God, they just have to walk this trail.
—— Diana Curry, a Mount Whitney dayhiker

I wake up before Mac's alarm goes off. Our tent door faces east. The morning light behind the Inyo Mountains glows red, pink, orange, blue. Not a cloud in the sky. *I love you sunrise.* I unzip the tent screen and sit in my sleeping bag, admiring the beauty and feeling small. *Thank you for this glorious day.* I lean outside and twist around to view Mount Muir, Keeler Needle and all of the other granite sculptures that tower above our tiny tent. I get up and walk around. It looks like I'm the first one up. Mac stirs and we shift into gear.

We skip a hot breakfast. I nibble on some GORP as I heat some water for coffee. Mac retrieves the marmot bag. I decide that a cup of tea would take too long to cool for me to drink, so I pass. We attend to our personal matters. I brush my hair and braid it. We dress. I fill my shirt pocket with lip balm, handkerchief, an extra hair tie, my small spiral notebook and a pen. Even though it's still a little chilly, I go for the shorts right away. As soon as we hit the trail, I'll get warm. We load the food we're taking, into our daypacks. I have two quarts of water and my 12-ounce personal bottle. Mac has three quarts and his 24-ounce personal bottle. Water is crucial up here. Water from here up is probably frozen. Mac packs the water filter to be safe.

The sun peeks over the distant mountains and smiles, encouraging us for the day. Two hikers start up the trail. *Darn, we're not the first.* We gracefully accept it. What choice do we have? Mac returns the marmot bag to its rock overhang and we secure the camp. Last minute check: water, water filter, food, maps, snacks, lunch, camera, binoculars, first aid kit, aspirin, moleskin, tape, trekking poles, lip balm, sunscreens, rain gear, fleece pullover, notepad, pen, flashlight, sunglasses, hat, bandana, lime, cigar and lighter. Ready. We've got it all. We hoist our daypacks onto our backs. How light they seem compared to our backpacks. This'll be wonderfully strange and liberating. We leave our tent and backpacks at camp.

Off we go over our rock berm, onto the trail. Campers skitter about retrieving marmot bags, attending to personal matters and securing camp. Some are still sleeping. We pass the last tent. 6:22 a.m.

Smooch, smooch, a good luck kiss. What a perfect morning. All blue up there; no clouds.

Up, up, up. The trail begins with a gradual climb. I take the lead. The snow runoff that was flowing yesterday is ice this morning, making some of the rocks and trail quite slick. I consciously choose to watch my footing, rather than the scenery. This is no time or place to mess up.

We're in the midst of the switchbacks. *Oops! I forgot to count.* Oh well, I am not going back. My heartbeat and breath accelerate. I'm so excited and must slow down my pace. We've got quite a climb ahead of us. Five miles up. Five miles back. I sip water constantly. Our elevation gain from Trail Camp is about 2400 feet to the summit. I do not want to get altitude sickness. With the sudden surge of exercise, a slight headache begins to move in. I immediately take two aspirins.

A young man walks quickly up the trail below us. He's wearing a ball cap and using a wooden walking stick. Little details like these, . . . simple things like a hat, water, daypack, or walking stick, may become a vital tool for survival up here.

Purple-blue flowers join us along the trail. I don't recall ever seeing these flowers before.

"Those must be the Sky Pilots," Mac responds to my thinking.

"They are so cute!"

"You think everything is cute."

"Everything *is* cute," I tumble back.

Sky Pilot, Polemonium eximium. *Flowers blue, fragrant, densely clustered in terminal globelike head; leaves basal, 1 to 4 inches (2.5 to 10 cm) long, crowded with numerous leaflets surrounding central vein; stem 4 to 12 inches (10 to 30 cm) tall. Sky Pilot is strictly an alpine plant, rarely growing below 10,000 ft (3050 m). It is usually found in rock crevices or among boulders on high ridges. Blooms June–August.*

— *A Sierra Club Naturalist's Guide to The Sierra Nevada*

The Sky Pilots cheerfully guide us up the trail. Who would have thought that amongst all of these hard, cold-looking rocks and boulders, delicate blue flowers would live and bloom? Other small plants and flowers show themselves briefly along the trail, but the Sky Pilot gardens gleefully cascade down the seemingly desolate terrain. With my attention wrapped up in carefully navigating each step through the rocky and icy trail, I stop occasionally to touch the flowers and look around at the scenery. I hike ahead of Mac, then stop. When he catches up, I start again.

We gain on the only hikers ahead of us: A man and a woman. He's leading and ahead of her for some time. He stops to let her catch up. She rests. They walk on. It's possible to observe them easily because of all the switchbacks. We catch up. They stop and engage in discussion. The other young man is catching up from below.

"Hi there," I say to the couple, finding it impossible not to. Mac is right behind me.

"Hey. This trail is pretty icy. I don't like the looks of that trail up there across snow," the woman includes us in their discussion.

"Don't go across the snow," Mac relays information. "The ranger told us not to. When you reach the snow, the trail goes to the left. Watch for the cairns. *Don't go across the snow,*" he reiterates. "We watched some hikers do it yesterday and it took them a long time. The ranger said the trail is kind of hard to find at that point, and it's shorter across the snow but very dangerous."

I remember seeing this woman last night and noting her camping attire: Purple tights, purple top, big, black shorts, and a floppy brown hat. She has a wonderful smile. Mac tells them the story of the young man we watched yesterday who took the shortcut down the snow chute. The young man on the trail behind us, passes. He's moving quickly, determined and capable.

"Hey, thank you," the woman says. "I was telling my husband I wouldn't go on if I had to cross that snow up there. Thanks." They let us go on ahead.

We take off again. "We may have saved their marriage," I comment to Mac. The solo young man is already a switchback ahead. Wow. Up, up, up. Focusing on the trail and exerting energy leaves little time for anything else. The muscles in my legs feel alive. They're working. They're happy. I switch hands occasionally with my trekking pole. I like to be an equal opportunity provider for both of my arms and legs. "This pole is worth every cent," I comment to Mac. He agrees. I was reluctant to use a trekking pole, thinking that it was important to keep my hands free in case I need them for balance or breaking a fall. Now I can't imagine hiking this climb, up or down, without it. When I turn a switchback, I change hands so the pole is on the cliff side. This provides balance, comfort and confidence.

My attention stays on each step, each rock, each switchback, each flower and each breath. I pause occasionally to catch my breath and gaze at the unbelievable beauty. The view changes the higher we walk. I let my mind wander.

We reach the snow. I don't see the trail and let Mac ahead of me. He spies the cairn higher up, and we do our first boulder scramble of the trail.

The trail resumes its familiarity. I look back to see if the couple saw where we went. I don't see them. Mac spots the solo young man, way up on top, a silhouette against the deep blue sky. While I was lost in thought we've gained a lot of altitude. We move on.

Soon the trail crosses the uppermost section of the snow chute. "I thought we weren't supposed to cross the snow." It's obvious that this is the only way. Mac is already halfway across. I take a deep breath and start walking. *Don't look down,* I hear from inside. If I fall I will slide down the snow chute and won't stop until I hit the rocks about 1,000 feet below. *Isn't there a different way?* The muddy trail gets more narrow. The snow has a hard crust of ice on the surface and my trekking pole won't penetrate. A pair of jagged rocks inhibit easy stepping. I stop. I feel fear. "I'm afraid," I announce.

"Don't be afraid," Mac coaches.

"But I am." Fear can impede my operating capabilities. My mind quickly scans a thought process: I've learned to let go of fear by riding my bicycle. If I ride down a very steep hill with fear, the body tenses and becomes rigid. If I'd hit a bump, in that tense state, it increases the possibility for injury. So I have learned to recognize, acknowledge, let go of the fear and turn it into love, the love of going down a hill on my bicycle, fast. Put the release process to work — acknowledge, identify, understand, accept the fear and let it go. Learn to love this moment. Read the terrain and run the route.

I take a deep breath, quickly process the five steps, compose my Self, and physically regroup. I cross the snow with no problem. I love overcoming fears! It's so liberating.

"Whoa!" I hear Mac let out a joyful cry. "What a view!"

Trail Crest? We're here already? We've walked 2.2 miles up a granite mountain. "Whoa," I repeat the sensation when I reach the spot. My breath stops. At this altitude with less oxygen, a *breathtaking moment* is a special event, emotionally and physically. "What a view!" The horizon opens up west across to the Great Western Divide, the Kaweah Ridge, Sequoia National Forest and Kings Canyon. More mountains, canyons, lakes, and trees. "Oh my! This was worth every step." We pause and let time cease.

Drink more water, a little voice suggests. I do. Turning around, I look back from where we've come. "Oh my! We did that." I grab Mac and hug. I feel so lucky to be here and so thankful to Mac for making it possible. He didn't carry me up the mountain, however, and I feel proud of my Self for having made the journey. I look back to check on the couple below. *She's not going to like that part.*

But it's not over. Now the trail winds around the west side of Mount Muir. The John Muir Trail will join us soon. The trail is supposed to level out for a while until we get closer to the summit. The summit is 2.5 miles from Trail Crest.

As we start around the west side, the air temperature cools down. The morning sun has not yet come to this side of the mountain. I stop and put on my fleece pullover. The trail is more narrow and rocky. This is not an easy trail. It's fun, it's challenging, but it's certainly not for the timid. I'm glad I spent so much time playing at tide pools when I was a kid, hopping boulders and climbing rocks. Much of my childhood was spent playing at the seashore and loving it. That's where we played tag and hide-and-go-seek. I'm quite at home here. The cliff to our west drops off dramatically. The recent Yosemite rock slide invades my awareness again. I quickly banish the thought to prevent fear from moving in. *Stay in the now.*

"Whoa! It's one breath-taking moment after the next up here!" We've come to a narrow walkway, open, with drops on both sides, like a bridge. We can see the wilderness to the west and the Whitney Trail, Lone Pine, Owens Valley, and the Inyo Mountains on the east. I feel no fear crossing the narrow walkways. I love it. I love the fact that I'm not afraid. Cautious and careful but not afraid. Enthused. This is grand! This is JOY!

We spot the John Muir Trail far below us and two humans walking by a lake. We easily identify Guitar Lake. Yesterday, the JMT hiker said it was much easier to come up Mount Whitney from the west side, but I don't see how.

The trail presents another narrow walkway with that incredible two-way view. And another. Thank goodness I'm not acrophobic.

Some backpackers come down from the summit. I ask, "Where did you hike from? How long did it take?"

"Tuolumne Meadows. Two weeks."

I ask *the* question, "What was your favorite part?"

The familiar look of memory and thought fills one's expression. His tanned skin smiles with miles. "The summit," he says without any more thought. "We spent the night there last night. What a view. We watched the sunset and the sunrise. What an experience."

We let them go and we walk on. The little blue Sky Pilots joyfully share the trail. I feel good. I'd break out in song if I could sing. Mac comments on the difficulty of the trail. I agree and watch my footing very carefully. I can't imagine some of the people we saw come down the trail yesterday, walking up this. How did they do it?

As we wind around a rock cliff we see Mount Whitney, far away, perched ever so majestically in the sky. "There it is! . . . . Oh my. We're going up there," never a question. We continue to plod along, taking our time to enjoy the view and drink water. I'm almost out of water. I'm down to my personal bottle. Both of my quarts are empty.

Two more backpackers come down, and then the young man who passed us first on the trail earlier this morning. Mac talks with him. I talk to the other backpackers. I can't believe how easy it's become to talk to total strangers. Ordinarily, (and climbing Mount Whitney certainly does not drop into the *ordinary* category) the process of initiating a relationship with a total stranger often takes a great deal of conversation to discover a common interest, experience, or passion. Up here it is very simple and easy.

After the young man passes, Mac stops, looks at me with a gleeful smile and says, "He said that we'll have it all to ourselves!"

"The summit?"

"There's nobody else up there. It'll be all ours, . . . for a bit," he reports.

This pleases Mac immensely. I love to see him so happy.

"We should probably put some of this snow in a water bottle," *O Practical One* says.

"Good idea."

He's reluctant to stop, even though he knows it is the practical thing to do. We need water. He is timing our hike to the summit and quite excited to be so close. I am happy to offer a sacrifice, "I'll gather some snow. You go on ahead."

He sparkles, "Are you sure?"

"Yeah. Go ahead. I'll be up as soon as I can." I read about gathering snow for drinking water. Here's what I remember: Stay away from colored snow. Don't eat snow or ice; it can reduce body temperature and could lead to dehydration. Let the snow melt. Then filter it. Boiling is good.

I pull out the wide-mouth Nalgene® quart bottle, open it, and try to scoop up some clean white snow. Ice covers the surface; it's not as soft as it looks. I break the surface and begin scooping. It takes a while. It takes a lot of scoops to fill up the quart. I thump the bottle on a rock to compress it. When it feels heavy, I close it, pack it away in my daypack, and fill another.

Up the trail I go into another switchback city. Mac is not too far above me. "Just follow the cairns." He's walking slower now. The climb is strenuous and the altitude slows me down. The trail is mostly rock. The only way to follow is by watching for the rock cairns that someone has lovingly nurtured. I find a cairn that has lost its top third rock and replace it.

I catch up to Mac.

"There it is!" Mac's voice sings joyfully when he sees the Smithsonian summit hut.

"It's bigger than I thought it would be and it's made out of stone. I don't know why, but I thought it was all metal." The hut, at the summit, was built in 1909 and the guidebook warns:

Do not seek shelter in the summit building. Its protection is merely imaginary and people have died "sheltering" themselves from lightning here. Get well down below the summit.
        — Mount Whitney—The Trail Route

Our pace quickens as our adrenaline flows.

"We did it!" we say together. We spin around and take in the view. Awesome.

"What time is it?" I check.

"Ten o'clock, exactly. Pretty good. Three hours and forty minutes. What a walk!"

The summit is not what I expected. I imagined it would be like a pointy peak with just enough room to lay a hand on the top rock, maybe hold onto a posted flagpole, flying the colors in the wind. Nope, nothing like that. We have plenty of room to walk around. Massive, flat rock slabs lie around piled on top of each other to make a huge deck. We hop from rock to rock. Distant snow-sprinkled peaks surround us. The day is perfectly clear and surprisingly warm. Not a cloud in the sky, no wind. The excitement of being up here warms my soul but I'll keep on my forest green fleece pullover, (a Mother's Day present from Jeremiah, thank you very much).

The summit hut is made of rock with a tin roof and a metal chimney poking up out of the south side. The windows are small and covered with hinged-metal plates. The register awaits. "Let's sign in."

The register is in a flat metal box sitting on the west side of the hut. I open the metal lid. Mac gets ready and says, "He didn't sign in. That guy didn't sign the register! I'll be the first one to sign in today, July 20."

I hold the lid up and see a stick inside that looks about the perfect size to prop the lid open and is.

"Here," Mac hands off the camera. "Would you take a picture of me signing it?"

Click. I do. He's so cute. My Sky Pilot. Thank you, Mac.

It's my turn to sign in. Mac wrote his entire name, *Michael James McDonald, "Mac."* I do the same: *Ellen Sherpa Pendleton, "esp."* Mac scurries to take a picture of me. I see the column headed, *Suggestions.* I write *Suggestions? This is perfect!* and add, *Thank you, Universe.*

We look at each other and break into spontaneous howling with all the air we can gather, then yell, "Top of the World, Ma!" We look at each other, smile, and hug. What a moment, . . . a breathtaking, nose tickling moment. Both of my ears tickle, too. Maybe it's the lack of oxygen. I like it. We grab our poles and walk around the hut. Mac finds a geological marker or some official plaque that is mounted in a big rock. I read it.

"Wait, I'll take a picture." Mac puts down his pole and daypack. I crawl up on the rock and lie next to the sign. *Click.* Then we switch and I take a picture of him doing the same. We leave our gear and walk over to the highest eastern edge, the true summit.

"Oh my," that's all I can say. We view in silence, taking it all in. The 360 degree panoramic view is amazing. Incredible. Awesome. Unbelievable. Mountains, mountains everywhere.

"One, two, three, four, five, six. I see six mountain ranges to the east." Peaks to the north, south, east, and west. Meadows, lakes, forests, more lakes. As far as my eye can see, landscape waiting for us to explore. We hold each other. "We did it." The light-headedness is not from the altitude; it is pure joy.

We take pictures of the other standing here and there. Every angle provides a spectacular backdrop. Pick one, any one.

Mac scrambles over to his pack. "I have to light a cigar." A few moments later he returns with the camera and a smoking stogie. "Here, would you take my picture?" He finds the right rock then postures up and turns his head to profile. *Click.*

"Great shot. Let's take another." He stands up and strikes another pose. "Turn your head so I can see the cigar," I suggest. He does. *Click.* "One more." He hops over the official Mount Whitney sign and snuggles up to it.

Click. Cigar Aficionado magazine centerfold. Mac's summit mission is complete.

I start walking toward the furthest eastern edge and find the perfect spot. Facing the Owens Valley and a vertical drop of the east face of who knows how many thousand feet, I open up and yell as loudly, slowly, and distinctly as I possibly can, . . ."HELLO, . . . WORLD. . . . THIS, . . . IS, . . . ELLEN, . . . PENDLETON, . . . AND, . . . EVERYONE, . . . BETTER, . . . JUST, . . . GET, . . . OUTTA, . . . THE, . . . WAY, . . . CUZ, . . . I'M, . . . COMING, . . . THROUGH!"

My body gasps for air.

I love it up here at the top of the world. No wind. I'm surprised. I thought I'd have to fight the wind to hold my ground. We drink some water, nibble some snacks, and sit on the cold rocks in the warm sun.

Mac gets up to explore the perimeter and the hut.

A hiker appears, walking toward the summit. A young man with seemingly ample energy, bounds straight for the edge.

"You did it!" I congratulate.

"Yes! I did it!" He faces the valley below, holds up both arms and unleashes a rowdy howl. Joy lights up his face. "I was born and raised in Lone Pine and this is my first trip to the summit. I am David." The well-earned pride of accomplishment blends gracefully with his happy energy.

I am proud of him too and have never met him before. "Ellen. Pleased to meet you. This is your first time?" I ask like an experienced old-timer.

"Yeah. I grew up here and never, ever felt the desire to climb it. My family owns a hotel in Lone Pine. I used to go fishing at Meysan Lake (great fishing there) but I never thought about going to the summit. I left Lone Pine for about ten years and now I'm back. All the kids who are born and raised here can't wait to leave town. Usually they never come back. I love Lone Pine. I went out there, into the world, and realized what a wonderful place this is." He turns around and yelps again.

The familiar couple trails up. I smile and they return it. We all have something in common. "Hi, there. You made it! Congratulations!" I feel like a self-appointed Mount Whitney welcome committee. "Do you have water? Want a snack?" (We have enough pretzels, trail mix, and peanut butter sandwiches for everyone.) They have their own and after the initial "o-o-o's" and "ah-h-h's" and picture taking, they join our picnic. "Would you like me to take a picture of you two together?" I offer. They take me up on it.

The conversations evolve. Scott and Karen from Danville. Some other folks know of Danville and they jump into the conversation.

"Monterey? We love Monterey. Scott lived there a couple of years while writing his thesis," Karen doing most of the talking.

"What was your thesis on?" I express interest.

Scott responds, rather quietly, "It had to do with lung conditions and degeneration."

Tuberculosis. Scott might be a doctor.

"My dad is coming up. It is his birthday today," Scott announces.

Peanut butter and jelly sandwiches taste exquisite up here. New folks to the summit arrive regularly. Someone says, "Hey, we've been out in the wilderness for a couple of weeks. Did anything happen while we were gone?"

"Did you hear about the TWA jet that blew up leaving New York City? JFK airport," someone reports.

This is news to us. We've been out of media contact for only five days and look what happens. On Mac's first backpack trip in 1991, when he got back to "civilization" the Gulf War had started. That was quite a shock.

I listen to a man talking to a couple of rock climbers. His accent sounds familiar. Finally I can't stand the suspense any longer, "Where is your accent from?"

The man blushes slightly and softly tells, "Maine."

"Maine! Mac's parents live in Maine."

"What city?" Mac enters the conversation.

"Etna."

"My parents live outside of Portland in Scarborough," Mac gives.

"Oh, I know where Scarborough is. I have a good friend who lives there. I'll be going there to pick up my red raspberries," his accent sounds fuller now, more comfortable, with more accent.

"I love your accent. We have a good friend, Jeff Whitmore, a writer, and his accent sounds something like yours. I love it!" I have to say.

"My parents live on Blackpoint Road," Mac continues.

"That's close to my raspberries." Mike from Maine has a ten-day beard and his clothes have probably been on him about the same length of time. He and his girlfriend, Carla, are here in California for a wedding in Fresno. They started hiking from Cedar Grove in Kings Canyon. They joined the John Muir trail somewhere along the way and they've been hiking about two weeks. They were advised to take Forester Pass but chose Harrison. They had a hard time and said next time they'd probably do Forester but, obviously, they made it. They're interested in talking to the rock climbers who just climbed up the Mountaineer's Route. They walk over to introduce themselves and immediately discuss an entertaining article written about climbing Mount Whitney that was published about a year ago in *Climbing* magazine or *Rock & Ice*. They had all read it, but none remembers in which magazine. They all laugh and say that it was pretty funny. I note to look it up when we get home.

I love listening to the couple from Maine talking to the rock climbers. They use terms that nearly convince me they're speaking a foreign language. When there's a break, (the climbers take a short nap) I jump in and invite Mike and Carla to visit Mac's parents if they get close to Scarborough. I write down their names, address, phone number and Mac's name. Mac's parents would get a great kick out of meeting someone who was there when their Number One Son stood on the summit of the highest peak in the forty-eight United States.

A lone marmot sniffs us out. Folks have come and gone up here on the summit. Twosomes, threesomes, and foursomes ask me to take their pictures. Cell phones are pulled out and passed around. One man leaves a message on the answering machine to his wife, who is due to have a baby at any moment. I take pictures of the entire assemblage.

Soon the rock climbers prepare for descent. Mike and Carla watch carefully. Their plan is to hike down to Whitney Portal, pick up their climbing gear, then come back up and rock climb the east face of Mount Whitney. The Mountaineer's Route is a different climb. I'm not a rock climber and can't imagine being a rock climber, so I don't pay too much attention. We walk over to the other side of the hut, past the "toilet" (a 5-gallon bucket on a platform surrounded by a brown, picket, two-sided screen), to the spot where the climbers start their descent.

"No ropes?" I was paying enough attention to hear this tidbit.

"No ropes. This is easy," a climber tells. Mike, Carla, and the climbers talk climbing talk.

"You just climb down there with no ropes," I spurt out finding it hard to believe. I find it hard to watch, too.

They back down the rocks, looking quite happy about it all, then disappear. I carefully peek over the edge.

Mike and Carla appear to be excited about the climb and quite confident. Carla started rock climbing two years ago and immediately got hooked.

I'd need a hook to keep from tumbling down.

"Shall we head back down?" Mac asks me.

"What time is it?"

"It's 1:15 . . . . We've been up here three hours. Do you believe that?"

It doesn't seem possible. My, my, where did the time go? We say our good-byes to Mike and Carla and invite them to stop by our tent at Trail Camp on their way down. It's hard to leave but we must.

"Okay, 1:19 p.m." The walk down is certainly different from the walk up. First of all, we have to pass all of the people who are still making their way up. Most of them look like walking zombies. Dayhikers. Then I see a familiar man in a straw hat. He seems to be doing better than most. I walk up to him and boldly ask, "Are you Mr. Gee?"

He lights up, catching his breath from the climb. "How did you know?"

"I heard about you in camp last night. *The 70 year-old man in the straw hat.* Happy birthday!"

"This is my seventh time up here. One time for each decade," he responds with a proud twinkle.

"I'm very pleased to meet you. I was talking to your son and his wife up here. Did they go back down?" referring to Scott and Karen.

"Yes. He's always got somewhere to go." The father wisely adds, "He's very busy. I'm just glad he could make it at all."

"Well, you're almost there. Congratulations and have fun!"

"Thank you. It was very nice to meet you. What is your name?"

"Ellen Pendleton."

"Pendleton. Nice to meet you."

I'd like to sit and talk with him the rest of the day. We let them go. The folks coming up are not in good moods. They look very hot and tired. They really look like zombies. Some of them are carrying only a small empty water bottle. They don't have daypacks or fanny packs at all. Hordes of zombie hikers pass us.

"Did we look like that on our way up?" Mac reflects.

"No. I don't think so. We hiked up while it was still cool. We weren't in the sun on the whole backside section." I turn back to say, "Thank you," and "farewell summit." I feel a special relationship with this granite mountain. I feel lucky and alive. I'm proud of Mac for doing his homework and being so practical and well prepared. We did the trip right. We didn't reach the summit as zombies. And I've learned that there's a difference between hiking and mountaineering to the summit of Mount Whitney. The rockers are amazing!

As we pass the JMT junction, I count ten packs leaning against the rock wall, apparently left by hikers from the JMT taking a side trip to the Mount Whitney summit. We pass Mount Muir, but don't take the time to scramble up to its summit, that looks quite different than Mount Whitney summit, not at all flat. I start to feel a slight headache and realize that I haven't been wearing my sunglasses. Mac teases me, saying I have altitude sickness, but I don't. I put on my sunglasses. The trail here is very rocky, with a sheer drop to the west. This narrow walkway would be real tricky with a full pack to carry. The views are breathtakingly gorgeous.

At Trail Crest, a number of people are stopped, taking in the view and resting. Some are going up, some down. One lady in a green fleece pullover sits perched atop a rock. She's beautiful with her long auburn hair swept up and rolled in a bun. She's slightly overweight and does not look like she feels very well right now.

"Are you okay?" I ask.

She smiles, nods, and thanks me for my concern.

Soon after Trail Crest and just before the snow crossing, Mac stops to put some moleskin on his two big toes. The downhill trek is creating some hot spots. It's better to take care of hot spots when you first feel them, rather than letting them develop into full-blown blisters. Folks pass us by going both ways. The lady in the green fleece pullover passes. She's carrying a paper shopping bag with handles. Hm-m-m. Mac comments on it. More people seem to be going down than up.

The snow crossing is easier now. The sun has melted the ice into slush. No problem. Down, down, down. I get into a "going downhill" rhythm and it feels good. I liberate my hand from the wristband of my trekking pole, to allow easier and faster hand-switching of the pole at every switchback. The lady in green, ahead of us, switchbacks below on the trail. The back of her neck has a nasty sunburn.

We get into a rhythm and start passing hikers. Finally, near the bottom, we catch up to the redhead and I offer, "The back of your neck looks really sunburned. Would you like some sunscreen?"

She declines, then thinks about it and accepts.

Mac checks his watch.

"Go ahead. I'll catch up," I know he's timing our descent.

He walks on.

I return my attention to the woman in green. She doesn't look well. "Do you have water?"

She pulls out a Nalgene® bottle with about three tablespoons of water in it. "A little. You know what I need?

Do you have any aspirin or Advil® or something like that? I started feeling really bad up there and sat down. I let my boyfriend go on to the summit; I couldn't go any further. I got a terrible headache, felt dizzy and nauseous."

"Altitude sickness. You did good, though. You got pretty far and it was wise not to go on. The best thing to do is to get to a lower elevation."

She hands back the sunscreen. We introduce ourselves and start walking down together trail chatting. Her name is Diana.

"I'm out of water, but I'll ask Mac if we can filter some for you. I took all of my aspirin but Mac probably has some Ibuprofen®."

Soon I see Mac perched on the rock where we started this morning at 6:22 a.m. He looks very happy and proud, . . . and should be. He did his homework. Everything was perfect.

On the way down the trail, we pass three young men, sitting, taking a rest. They seem to be in good physical shape, buffed but over-tanned by the sun. I hear them talking about being out of water. I choose not to stop and offer Mac's water filter again.

We reach Mac at 4:22 p.m. He touched the rock at 4 p.m. Three hours down for me. He has one more Ibuprofen® left and gives it to Diana. She's from St. Thomas in the Virgin Islands, a teacher in a mountain village and has 25 students of all ages. She's been on a whirlwind travel trip and said the jet lag probably didn't help the altitude sickness. She has a lovely smile. I set her down at the rock wall next to the trail so her boyfriend can't miss her when he hikes through. Mac runs off and filters some water for her. She shades her head and waits.

"Did you come up today from Whitney Portal?" hoping they hadn't.

"No. We're camped just above Mirror Lake."

"Are you hungry?" I ask.

"I'm a vegetarian and my boyfriend left me with salami and a tuna fish sandwich. I ate the sandwich and that's when I started feeling real bad. I don't eat sugar or chemicals. You might not have anything I can eat."

"How about an energy bar?"

"Does it have milk products in it? I'm lactose intolerant."

Mac shows up with full water bottles. After giving her directions to our tent site, I head back to begin dinner preparations.

Home. The marmots didn't ransack our packs. Camp is how we left it this morning. I transfer the daypack contents back into my backpack. Mac joins me. We celebrate our success with a kiss and a hug. What a great day. Mac retrieves the marmot bag then gathers the empty water bottles, the filter, and walks to the pond. I follow and get a pot full of water for tea, then check on Diana.

When Mac returns with the water, he sets up a little spot with his Therm-a-Rest® and pulls out the binoculars to watch the hikers on the switchbacks. The Rosy finches show up again. Trail Camp entertainment.

Diana and her boyfriend, Mike, find us. Mike looks a little weather worn. They both do. They're out of water and he left his water filter in his truck back down at Whitney Portal. They borrow our filter. Mac shows them his favorite spot at the pond and gives them an extra water bottle.

As dinner cooks, Mike and Diana return the water filter and give us plenty of thanks. We invite them for dinner but they're eager to get back to their camp. We bid *adieu*.

Appetizers: Hummus and whole wheat tortillas. Dinner: Cup-of-soups, macaroni and cheese. Sounds simple but it's nummy. Almost anything would taste great up here.

I'm getting pretty good at the backpacking dish washing technique. I heat some water on the little stove and carry it over to the designated dishwashing rock. M-m-m-m. Feels good on the hands.

Mac watches hikers as they continue to descend the mountain. "Hey. Look at these. They're skipping the switchbacks. They're going straight down. No, they're stopping, sitting, talking. What are they doing?"

Mac offers the binoculars and I get involved. "It's those young women we passed up near the summit. Remember the one in the big hat? They were memorable zombies even back then. How long have they been up there?" We passed them at about 1:30 or 2 p.m. and they were a mess then. It's 7:30 now. I hand the binoculars back to Mac and he follows their wanderings, giving me the play-by-play action.

When they finally get down off the switchbacks, Mac says, "I have to go down to the trail and see this." We cross over our rock barrier and take up residence on a big sitting rock that's between the trail and the solar latrine. Mac figures they're sure to stop here.

Sure enough, they stop. We talk. They don't have flashlights, map, water or food. They are really disoriented. Two young women and a young man. Their English isn't the best but it's good enough. Mac talks with them.

I strike up conversation with a teenage boy who is hanging out by the latrine trying to sneak a smoke while away from his dad. He's from just north of New York City where he lives with his mom. He's visiting his dad in Los Angeles. This is their big adventure, carrying a 45-pound pack six miles up a mountain. Dad shows up, dressed in movie company logo jacket and hat. Dad carried a 65-pound pack up here. That doesn't sound like much fun. They had planned to summit then exit through Cottonwood Lakes/Horseshoe Meadow area about 30 walking miles to the south, where they've arranged with someone to pick them up. They're considering changing their plan. They're exhausted. The boy is okay, he just wants his cigarette.

Mac continues conversing with the three dayhikers. "We stashed our flashlights somewhere along the trail," the male of the group confesses. "It's by a lake . . . and there's a big, flat rock . . . and lots of tall, green trees with red bark."

It's eight o'clock and getting dark. They have six miles of trail to get to Whitney Portal. At least they have jackets. Mac talks to them for a bit, offering verbal directions down the mountain. They leave.

"Whoa! I don't believe them. They don't have a clue. I hope they make it to their flashlights," Mac shows disbelief and great concern.

We sit on the rock by the trail and talk to the man and his son. A woman and her son, who I recognize from the summit, stroll over to use the latrine. The boy is walking slower than before. He looks tired.

"Congratulations!" I say, still in my welcoming committee mode. "You did it! How old are you?"

"Thirteen."

"Well, you should be proud of yourself. You did a great thing," offering praise and encouragement.

"Thanks," he returns with a slight blush. His mom appears to be quite proud of both of them.

He takes the toilet paper from his pocket and climbs the stairs. Mom hangs out with us. We continue talking about the three who just left and how ill-prepared most of the dayhikers seem to be.

Oh people, people. I'm glad I'm with *O Practical One,* who read all the books, did all of his homework, and prepared for anything that might happen up here in the High Sierra. Many dayhikers, guilty of an amusement park mentality, think they can get off the ride at anytime. The wilderness is just that, wild. We haven't seen a ranger all day.

We talk and trash the dayhikers. Then, much to our surprise, coming back up the trail appear the three who just left. The three who stashed their flashlights, somewhere. The male speaks to Mac, "Can you take us in for the night?"

Mac had probably said in his parting words, " . . . if there's anything we can do . . ." that they have taken literally. I do a mental inventory of my backpack and wonder if I accidentally packed an extra sleeping bag or two? or blankets? or tent? . . . . Nope.

Mac is as shocked as the rest of us. "We don't have any room. We've got a two-person tent and two sleeping bags."

I turn away, amazed at the idea of "putting up" three extra persons in our tent tonight. They *must* be totally disoriented. Mac continues to talk with them. I resume talk with the other folks, turning away from the three dayhikers to hide my smirky, self-satisfied grin. I'm ashamed of the feeling and embarrass myself but I can't believe they have the audacity to ask us to bail them out of this preventable predicament.

Mac asks me, "Flashlight. Can we spare a flashlight?" I follow him to our tent site. He doesn't want to donate his brand new headlamp. I retrieve my extra flashlight and return to the threesome. Mac also sacrifices a keychain-squeeze-model flashlight, refills their water bottle, throws in some trail mix and a map. He's a saint. He offers more verbal directions and sends them on their way. We both feel bad about not being able *to take them in,* and had it been a life-or-death situation, such as bad weather or injury, certainly we would have. But this is not the case. They somehow didn't realize that a 22-mile hike with a 6,100-foot elevation gain might take a bit longer than they thought. Mac and I could spend a lot of time and gear saving Mount Whitney dayhikers.

"I hope we don't find them in the morning huddled up together somewhere along the trail, frozen to death," Mac feels bad.

"I couldn't believe last night," the 13-year-old's mother starts. "Last night, at ten o'clock, a young man stood outside of my tent. 'Wake up,' he yelled. 'I'm cold and hungry.' I unzipped the tent and he stood there in a T-shirt, shivering. No jacket, no flashlight, no water, no food. 'Can I sleep in your tent with you?' I couldn't believe it. It was just my son and me in a two-person tent. There was no way I was going to let him in. I sent him down to the Boy Scouts who had already taken in some other people. Dayhikers came down the trail all night."

We all decide we'd better move away from the trail before anyone else stops and asks for help.

Two backpackers pass by on their way down the trail. No headlamps. They don't stop. They're walking at a good pace. "Maybe they'll help the other three down the trail," Mac whispers, genuinely concerned and feeling responsible.

I hope they make it okay, for their sake and his. We turn in and sit in the tent trying to imagine where we would have put three more people. Fortunately our tent site is over a rock berm and cannot be seen from the trail. We're safely out of sight. It's been quite a glorious day. Thank you.

July 21, Sunday ○♎
Mount Whitney ~ Day Six

Go confidently in the direction of your dreams! Live the life you've imagined. As you simplify your life, the laws of the universe will be simpler.

— Henry David Thoreau

The dawn awakes to another perfect day. Not one cloud. I don't know words to describe the colors of this morning light. I give up trying to find them and enjoy the view. The morning air is fresh and crisp. I go out to play.

Still in the tent, Mac exercises his creativity and humor by composing a sacrilegious symphony, *Salute to the Sun.* He performs this using the excess flatulence one sometimes experiences at these higher altitudes. *Ode to the Satiated Marmot,* comes next.

Breakfast is leisurely. Campers stir, some getting ready to ascend the 96 or 97 switchbacks, some getting ready to leave the mountain. Mac asks, "Did you see the joggers?"

I catch sight of two tiny figures running up the switchbacks. "Oh, my! Are they crazy?" It would be easy to stay up here another day and enjoy ourselves but we do have to get back to The Other World. I won't call it the *real* world because this seems far more real to me than what we call civilization. I love it up here.

We pack up and hoist our loads onto our backs, securing our hip belts and making adjustments. I don't want to leave. This day will go by too quickly. "Good-bye, Whitney. Thank you." We ask a passer-by for a favor and hand him the camera: One last picture of us with Whitney in the background. I feel a smile all around.

Down we must. Two poles would be great going down. It would probably help take the impact off of the knees. One really helps but two would be better. No trees up here to snag a fallen branch.

We backtrack to Trailside Meadow where the Sierra Shooting-stars greet us. Backpackers and hikers come up the trail. I smile, thinking of the adventures they will have and the stories they will tell. We hike down past memories. Consultation Lake and the bagpiper magic. The Last Tree is now the First Tree. Mirror Lake, probably the scene of many stashed and lost flashlights. Outpost Camp, we stop for a break. I wish we were going back up. Bighorn Park and the quiet, gentle sweet shadow of the forest that means soon we'll see Lone Pine Lake. I should be happy to see it but I'm not; it means we are nearer to the end. Mac becomes barn sour but I stroll, enjoying the view. These lupines are almost as tall as me.

The trail grows wider with more and more hikers coming up. An older couple approaches. The woman is wearing a hat with huge sunflowers perched on the front brim. "Hi," I smile. They have backpacks and look like they might spend a lot of time outdoors. He's tanned and they both appear to be in great physical shape. She's styling with the hat and stands out. "Going to the summit?"

They stop and smile. She says, "Yes, we're doing the John Muir Trail. We dropped down into Lone Pine for supplies. Nice little town."

We trail chat for a bit then move along. Her hat cheers me up and their age inspires. How nice to be in your Golden Years and cruising through the Sierra with the one you love. I hope I'll be backpacking for a long, long time.

We're almost there. A hot shower starts sounding REALLY good. No wonder Mac got barn sour. My pace quickens. I feel great. My body is tight and efficient. I'm very lucky to have this wonderful, healthy body. *Thank you, Body. Thank you for taking me up there. Awesome trip!*

An adult with a line of children pass by. Five, six, seven. All different. At the end is a chubby little girl struggling to keep up. She has the most beautiful long red hair that I have ever seen and I spontaneously announce as such. She stops and her struggle becomes a smile. Her body grows tall and she knows that everyone in line before her heard the compliment and wanted one too. This child is special.

Any fear of bear damage is extinguished as we find the car and count the healthy windows and doors.

Everything is intact, unscathed. We drop our packs and try to remember how to do this reality part. Car keys. Mac has it together. We put our packs in the car, take off our boots, replace them with flip-flops and grab our After Trail Bags full of clean clothes and shower stuff. This shower can't happen soon enough. We wander toward the Whitney Portal Store to find out if it can happen at all.

"Yes, we're in," Mac reports. "And this was left for me." He holds a zip-lock baggie. In it is his map, two flashlights and a napkin. He opens it up to find a note written on the napkin:

> Mac,
> Thank you so much for your generosity. The flashlight helped us get to our own flashlights that we had hid along the trail. Our friends waited for us there and took us down. All and all, we had an experience of a lifetime. Thank you.
> — The 3 Whitney Survivors

Amazing! One, they made it. Two, they put together this baggie. Three, we got it. Will wonders never cease? We take our towels and make our way around the back of the store. We have to squeeze around a corner and a rock, "Now, he said it's not the best, but he assured me it's clean." We open the door and yes, it's rather funky. BUT, . . . is there hot water? It smells of disinfectant and the decor is early plastic BUT, . . . yes, . . . hot water. The shower stall is not big enough for both of us so I let Mac go first. He wastes no time. I take out my braid and brush my hair. Mac moans and groans with sensual delight. My time will come.

The day is only half gone and what a wonderful day it has been. We still have a long drive ahead of us, about 400 miles.

My turn. Ahhhhhhhhh. Yes! Yes! Heaven! Oh my, this makes the day even better. Wow! The wonders of technology – hot running water. I do my thang and join Mac outside. I look up at the deep blue sky and three little clouds float by. "Those are the first clouds we've had since we started. Thank you, Clouds. Perfect."

I see someone familiar. "Mr. Gee! Happy Birthday, again!"

He smiles. His family surrounds him sitting on a bench in the shade. "Thank you. We made it."

"Mr. Gee, what was your favorite part of the trip?" I ask as I have asked many others.

Without hesitation he twinkles and says, "The whole thing, every bit of it!"

My answer too.

As we wander back to the car taking one more look at it all, a backpacking couple getting ready to hit the trail yells, "Mac! Ellen!" Mike and Carla stand donned with their climbing gear ready to go back up. "Fancy meeting you here." We chat for a bit, take pictures and wish each other a safe and fun journey. Oh how I wish I were going back up.

7/18 Whitney Portal to Outpost Camp-8:30am-11:20am=2 hrs.50min. 3.5 miles
7/19 Outpost Camp to Trail Camp - 7:30am-11:05am = 3 hrs. 35 min. 2.5 miles
                                         Bagpiper break = 30 min.
7/20 Trail Camp to summit -   6:22am - 10:00am = 3 hrs. 40 min. 4.7 miles
Summit to Trail Camp-   1:19pm - 4:00pm = 2 hrs.40 min. 4.7 miles
7/21 Trail Camp to Whitney Portal -8:45am - 11:50am = 3 hrs. 5 min. 6.0 miles
                                   Total time = 16 hrs. 20 min. 21.4 miles

So in a perfect world if you leave Whitney Portal at 4 a.m., stop ½ hour for lunch, spend ten minutes at the summit, and ½ hour filtering water or taking potty breaks, you'd get back to Whitney Portal at about 9:30 p.m., providing you're in great shape, don't get altitude sickness and nothing happens to you along the way. The novice dayhiker should take a jacket, hat, rain gear, flashlights, food, matches, a knife, sunglasses, water filter, moleskin, sunscreen, aspirin, map, and a first aid kit. No less. Experts can make their own decisions.

While driving south on Highway 395 headed home, clouds become the main attraction. I'm amazed that we haven't seen clouds since we left home and now, as our adventure comes to its end, clouds decorate the sky and suggest rain. We have truly been blessed on this trip. *Thank you, Universe. I appreciate the impeccable details that you create and orchestrate.*

On my next backpack adventure with Mac, I'd like to go without crowds of people. I'm ready to experience that. However, this trip was filled with memorable characters: Tom the bagpiper from Toronto, Lone Pine David, Karen and Scott from Danville, Mr. Gee, the 13 year-old boy, Mike and Carla from Maine, Diana from the islands, the *3 Whitney Survivors*, the older JMT couple (the lady with the sunflowers on her hat), and the little girl with the pretty red hair. These are faces of people I will remember. We shared a piece of Earth. We each shared a piece of ourselves. We shared a mountain.

I feel differently now. I have walked the walk to the summit of a 14,496 foot mountain, opened up my heart and voice to the entire universe . . . filled with JOY . . . smiled the smiles . . . held the man I love . . . all from the summit of the highest peak around. What a feeling. What a view. What a summit. I'm a lucky soul. I love being human.

It's 5 p.m. Mac is driving. We're listening to U2, *Joshua Tree*, in honor of all the Joshua trees here in this desert. The temperature is at least 100. The sun beats down on us. To put on the car's air conditioner is something neither of us wants to do, hoping to preserve our "naturalness" as long as possible. The wind and the heat have priority. They are Mother Nature, gifts from God. The clouds that are between us and the sun are glowing colors: blues, reds, greens. Rainbows, but no rain. If I could paint a picture of the mountains, the sky, clouds, rainbows, and sun right now, it would look unreal. The beauty humbles me.

I love Planet Earth. What a glorious place to be. There's so much of it yet to see. How am I possibly going to see it all? Reincarnation? I am eager to explore the wilderness, climb more mountains, hug more trees, touch more flowers and watch more sunrises.

We reach Walker Pass. Unlike previous drives over Walker Pass, Mac seems interested this time. He pulls off the highway onto a dirt road and we find a PCT trailhead campground. Do I see another adventure in the making? Oh JOY, . . . RAPTURE! I feel curious, brand new, and eager to be back *out there*, . . . soon. Namaste.

RESOURCES

BOOKS BY AUTHOR

Abbey, Edward, *Down the River*, E.P. Dutton, Inc., 2 Park Avenue, New York, NY 10016. 1982

Agee, Doris, *Edgar Cayce on ESP*, Warner Books, 75 Rockefeller Plaza, New York, NY 10019. 1969

Axcell, Claudia, Diana Cooke, Vikki Kinmont, *Simple Foods for the Pack*, Sierra Club Books, 730 Polk Street, San Francisco, CA 94109. 1986

Carrighar, Sally, *Home to the Wilderness – A Personal Journey*, Penguin Books, 625 Madison Avenue, New York, NY 10022. 1978

Carson, Rachel, *Silent Spring*, Houghton Mifflin, 215 Park Ave. South, New York, NY 10003. 1962

Cassady, Jim, Bill Cross, Fryar Calhoun, *Western Whitewater, From the Rockies to the Pacific*, North Fork Press, P.O. Box 3580, Berkeley, CA 94703-0580. 1994

Dalai Lama, *Freedom in Exile, Autobiography of the Dalai Lama*, HarperCollins Publ., 10 East 53rd Street., New York, NY 10022. 1990

Dillard, Annie, *Pilgrim at Tinker Creek*, A Bantam Book, Harper & Row, Publishers Inc., 10 East 53rd Street, New York, N.Y. 10022. 1979

Fleming, June, *Staying Found*, The Mountaineers, 1001 SW Klickitat Way, Seattle, WA 98134. 1994

Fletcher, Colin, *The Complete Walker III*, Alfred A. Knopf, Inc., New York, NY. 1987

Fletcher, Colin, *The Man Who Walked Through Time*, Vintage Books, Random House, New York, NY. 1972

Fletcher, Colin, *The Thousand-Mile Summer*, Howell-North Books, Berkeley, CA. 1964

Goulart, Frances Sheridan, *The Caffeine Book: A User's and Abuser's Guide*, Dodd, Mead & Co. Inc., 79 Madison Avenue, New York, NY 10016. 1984

Hellweg, Paul, and Scott McDonald, *Mount Whitney Guide for Hikers and Climbers*, Canyon Publishing Co., 8561 Eatough Ave., Canoga Park, CA 91304. 1994

Houston, Jeanne Wakatsuki and James D. Houston, *Farewell to Manzanar*, Bantam Books, Houghton Mifflin Co., 2 Park St. Boston, MA 02107. 1985

Hurston, Zora Neale, *Their Eyes Were Watching God*, Quality Paperback Books, New York, NY. 1990

Irwin, Sue, *California's Eastern Sierra, A Visitor's Guide*, Cachuma Press, P.O. Box 360, Los Olivos, CA 93441. 1991

Leo, Richard, *Way Out Here – Modern Life In Ice-Age Alaska*, Sasquatch Books, 1008 Western Ave., Seattle, WA 98104. 1996

Muir, John, *My First Summer in the Sierra*, Sierra Club, 730 Polk Street, San Francisco, CA 94109. 1988

Peterson, Roger Tory, *A Field Guide to Western Birds*, Riverside Press, Cambridge MA. 1961

Ross, Cindy, *Journey on the Crest*, The Mountaineers, 1001 SW Klickitat Way, Seattle, WA 98134.

Rowell, Galen, and Dalai Lama, *My Tibet*, A Mountain Light Press Book, University of California Press, Berkeley & Los Angeles, CA. 1990

Secor, R.J., *High Sierra – Peaks, Passes, and Trails*, The Mountaineers, 1001 SW Klickitat Way, Seattle, WA 98134. 1992

Stienstra, Tom, *California Camping: The Complete Guide*, Foghorn Press, 555 DeHaro Street #220, San Francisco, CA 94107. 1994

Stienstra, Tom and Michael Hodgson, *California Hiking: The Complete Guide*, Foghorn Press, 555 DeHaro Street #220, San Francisco, CA 94107. 1994

Strauss, Robert, *Adventure Trekking. A Handbook for Independent Travelers*, The Mountaineers, 1001 SW Klickitat Way, Seattle, WA 98134. 1996

Storer, Tracy I., and Robert L. Usinger, *Sierra Nevada Natural History*, University of California Press, Berkeley and Los Angeles, CA. 1963

Tompkins, Peter, and Christopher Bird, *The Secret Life of Plants*, Harper and Row, Publications, Inc., 10 East 53rd Street, New York, NY 10022. 1974

Whitney, Stephen, *The Sierra Nevada: A Sierra Club Naturalist's Guide*, Sierra Club Books, 730 Polk Street, San Francisco, CA 94109. 1979

Wood, Robert S., *The 2 oz. Backpacker*, Ten Speed Press, P.O. Box 7123, Berkeley, CA 94707. 1982

Yogananda, Paramahansa, *Autobiography of a Yogi,* Crystal Clarity Publishers, 14618 Tyler Foote Road, Nevada City, CA 95959. 1995

BOOKS BY TITLE

Audubon Field Guide to North American Wildflowers, The, Alfred A. Knopf, Inc., New York, NY 10019. 1979

Concise Columbia Encyclopedia, The, Avon Books, The Hearst Corp., 1790 Broadway, New York, NY 10019. 1983

Mount Whitney – The Trail Route, Sierra Nevada Peak Guides

Popular Outings of the Monterey Bay Area and Beyond, Ventana Chapter of the Sierra Club, P.O. Box 5667, Carmel, CA 93921-5667. 1993

MAGAZINES

Backpacker, Rodale Press, Inc., 33 E. Minor Street, Emmaus, PA 18098

CitySports, Competitor, Inc., 214 South Cedros Avenue, Solana Beach, CA 92075. July 1995

Monterey County Weekly, Milestone Communications, Inc., 668 Williams Avenue, Seaside, CA 93955

Outdoor Photographer, Werner Publishing Corp., 12121 Wilshire Blvd., Suite 1220, Los Angeles, CA 90025-1175

Ventana, The, The Ventana Chapter of the Sierra Club, P.O. Box 604, Santa Cruz, CA 95061

NEWSPAPERS

San Francisco Chronicle, 901 Mission Street, San Francisco, CA 94103-2988. *Tone Deaf* in "Earth Week" section, July 22, 1995

The Monterey County Herald, P.O. Box 271, Monterey, CA 93942

AUDIOBOOKS

Fletcher, Colin, *Learn of the Green World,* Audio Press, Louisville, CO. 1991

MISCELLANEOUS

Backcountry Basics, Sequoia & Kings Canyon National Parks, US Dept. of the Interior, NP Service, Three Rivers, CA 93271

Celestial Influences calendar, Quicksilver Productions, P.O. Box 340, Ashland OR 97520 *www.quicksilverproductions.com*

Echo River Trips, 116 Oak Street, Suite 1, Hood River, OR 97031. (800)652-3246 *www.echotrips.com*

Larson, Gary, *The Far Side,* Universal Press Syndicate Company, 4400 Johnson Drive, Fairway, Kansas 66205

Mac's Field Guide, The Mountaineers, 1011 SW Klickitat Way, Seattle, WA 93134. 1991

Mount Whitney – The Trail Route, Sierra Nevada Peak Guides, Eastside Desktop Publishing, Route 1 Box 58, Mammoth Lakes, CA 93546. 1991

National Parks of the World *www.NationalParks-World.com*

Tom Harrison maps, 2 Falmouth Cove, San Rafael CA 94901-4465 *www.tomharrisonmaps.com*

AUTHOR
Ellen Pendleton
www.EllenPendleton.com
www.Earth-Travels.net ~ Read & Run
Take A Hike
Thank you for your time and HAPPY TRAILS

ZODIAC SYMBOLS

Sun	☼
Moon	☽
Aries	♈
Taurus	♉
Gemini	♊
Cancer	♋
Leo	♌
Virgo	♍
Libra	♎
Scorpio	♏
Sagittarius	♐
Capricorn	♑
Aquarius	♒
Pisces	♓

Now, . . .

go outside

and play!

The world is not to be put in order, the world is order incarnate. It is for us to put ourselves in unison with this order.

— Henry Miller

And I admire writers so much. Writing a book is hard, even a bad book; writing a good book is impossible. It's like meeting real magicians and knowing there are no wires or secret pockets, that all the tricks are acts of will.

— Jon Carroll

Do you open books from the back? Me too. Welcome.

Made in the USA
Charleston, SC
05 November 2013